This book remembers
Sinyati Lebene, Godfrey Musaka,
Catalina Quispe, Beatrice Lubega,
and hundreds of others we met
in the poor countries.
Their bravery and humanity
have inspired
those with whom they live and work,
and touched us with humility and respect.

Jim Klobuchar and Susan Wilkes

Contents

A Thought for the Reader

If you believe that the insecurity America feels today is connected with the vast and widening chasm between the world's rich nations and poor nations, then you'll want to know that this fear can be reduced.

If you believe human beings were not intended to live like animals, as nearly a billion do today, then you are a person who will want to know what you can do to change their lives.

If you believe we can make friends and business partners of millions of people who are ambitious but happen to be poor, then you will want to know that the microcredit movement has already done this with extraordinary success in some of the poorest places on earth. It is not *the* answer to world poverty and the alienation it breeds, but it is a very important answer, endorsed and supported by prestigious foundations and corporate leaders.

This book tells how loans as small as $35 to $50, made through private or non-government groups throughout the world, have lifted scores of millions out of deepest poverty, empowered women, saved uncounted lives and built new ones.

It tells how with no great outlay of money you can be involved personally, irrespective of government policies you believe are misguided. It tells how you can make a transforming difference in one life or more, and what gifts that brings to those lives and to yours. This book shares with you the stories of some of those lives, and at the end offers a spectrum of providers for you to consider. It is a gateway for you to give a life to people who are voiceless but waiting for a chance to work their way out of oblivion.

Jim Klobuchar and Susan Wilkes

Preface

Let's be honest—what can a loan of less than $100 do, even in the hands of a persosn with integrity and ambition.

I know of one case in which a goodwill gesture by a friendlly landlord—the "loan" of $55 in the form of deferred rent—gave a young man the startup capital needed to found his business. A business which eventually grew into the 140-nation, multi-billion dollar enterprise that is today's Carlson Companies.

The year was 1938 and that young man was my father. While $55 would be a slightly larger amount in today's terms, it is the story—not the sum—that is important: an honest person with a good idea and a hard work ethic can't find a backer in traditional banks and lenders (no one would lend my father the money, either) but undaunted, the person eventually finds a modest amount of capital, takes the seed of an idea and turns it into a forest.

This age-old story is being played out again and again all over the world, by men and women who are searching only for small amounts of capital to fund a dream and lift them and their families out of abject poverty. It is the story of our own country, and the very foundation of the freedom and democracy in which we believe.

The "Miracles of Barefoot Capitalism" explores and documents the incredible power of the micro-lending phenomenon, especially as it applies to helping women who often live in societies where a women's role is still undervalued. As the authors note, "If a social evangelist had a choice of picking one tool, one movement with the goal of emancipatiing the poorest women on earth, the microcredit phenomenon wins without serious competition."

One may be tempted to think of the "miracle" of barefoot capitalism as being the loan recipient's achievement in the face of hardship. However, the true miracle here is that people in developed nations—like you and me—can make such an incredible impact on the world's future for such a small outlay of money and caring.

The movement took flight in the 1970s when Muhammed Yunus, an economics professors in Bangladesh, reached into his own pockets and loaned a total of $30 to 42 women in a small village who needed the cash to buy more material to make more bamboo stools. You'll read Mr. Yunus' story and many others.

Such as Scott Hillstrom and Eva Ombaka, who transformed $3500 into a chain of mini-pharmacies in the poorest regions of Kenya.

And Samya Abd Aelazeen, who began a dress making business in Egypt with the purchase of two sewing machines and a loan totalling less than $1000.

And the women in Samara, in eastern Russia, who grew a series of $65 loans into a number of shops in that region.

The stories in the book are numerous, the results truly inspiring.

I applaud Jim Klobuchar and Susan Wilkes for capturing the spirit of micro-lending and barefoot capitalism, and for opening readers' eyes to just how simple it is to participate and what a wonderful track record and global network there is behind the phenomenon.

Whether it's Minneapolis in the 1930s or Bangladesh in the 1970s, the power of a personal dream—given even a modicum of outside support—is the same: unstoppable. The story of microlending and Barefoot Capitalism is one which needs to be told often and to all who will listen. This book will help tremendously in that important effort.

So make yourself comfortable, and take off your shoes and get started.

Marilyn Carlson Nelson
Chairman and CEO
Carlson Companies

Foreword

They congregate each day in the conference rooms of hundreds of American newspapers and television channels. They come with computer printouts and bullet digests of what's happened around the world in the last 12 hours or the last 10 minutes. This is a news huddle and these are the editors and directors. The subject: what are the stories today, local, national and global, today's calamities, threats of war, triumphs and scandals? What goes on the front page or at the head of the newscast? The news gurus go down the list—the Middle East, weapons of mass destruction, crime, politics.

Somebody mentions Africa. "What's new in Africa?"

"The same," a voice says. "AIDS. Corruption. Civil war. Starving kids."

That was the answer for more than a decade. It got old and repugnant. Masses of TV watchers and newspaper readers tuned it out. These were people whose lives had no more room for stories of far-off AIDS or far-off tribal war. They tuned out news from Africa with a sigh of boredom. It expressed their futility. They were asking a question: How or why would you try to rescue those places? How can you understand them?

It was a predictable response after all of those years of slaughter and disease and overthrows and generic racketeering in government and the disappearance of some of our foreign aid, meager as that was. There wasn't much more shock left in the tragic story of Africa, and we didn't want to hear any more of it. But because we didn't, we might have missed—and are still missing—the beginning of another Africa. To Africa you can add South America and Central America, India, Indonesia, Bangladesh, the Philippines, Eastern Europe—the whole struggling developing world, what we once called "The Third World."

Tens of millions of people in places such as those, so often the scenes of tragedy and human despair, are finding a way to lift themselves out of poverty.

They don't ride on the magic carpet of mythology. Their vehicle is the humble small loan, as little as $35, and the password to their new lives is "microcredit."

The uplift of millions of poor around the world is still dogged by sickness, civil wars, and political and turf wars, as well as clinging poverty, and the story is fragmented. Our image of what we daintily call "developing" countries is dominated by the face of poverty and the sounds of political tumult. Because it is, we tend not to be aware of a changing face of those poor societies. It is a stirring, growing picture of people reaching beyond the turmoil. There are places where their story is powerful enough to bring tears. In this book you will meet people whose numbers run into the millions and who were all but abandoned. But today they are building new lives and often doing it with a buoyancy and camaraderie that can startle a visitor whose mind is programmed with images of a land helpless in the grip of epidemic and anarchy.

Small loans in themselves are no fresh discovery. But what's dramatically different is the concept of a structured and disciplined microcredit, or small loans made available to the poor. They're made possible at the outset by donor money from foundations, individuals, world bodies, and a range of nonprofit, governmental, and financial institutions in the industrialized countries. The goal of this credit system is to eventually make the borrowing groups in the poor countries self-sufficient, free of dependency on their subsidizers. Many already are. Today, in a little more than 30 years after the microcredit idea began taking hold, nearly 40 million small enterprisers in poor countries around the world are bringing better lives to their families. When you add the family members who benefit directly, the total mounts into the hundreds of millions. Thousands of lives have been saved. That is a phenomenon, and these are demonstrable figures.

It is happening today. Among the many remarkable sides to the story of microcredit is the fact that multitudes in America and the industrial west have never heard about it, at least in an identifiable form. Microcredit as a term does not exactly fill the air with electricity. But what it means is that people around the world who were once denied the most basic access to banking and to money that they could work with are now receiving credit. And amazingly, they are proving to be the best loan risks on earth.

Those small loans are created with money made available by a network of nonprofit organizations and government agencies throughout the world that insist on repayment and strict accounting. Those tiny businesses are fundamentally family businesses. The great majority of the borrowers are women—mothers who turn their small profits directly back to the family. Their loans will enable them to make woven baskets in Bolivia, to buy and fatten a cow on the Maasai Steppes in Africa, or to run a flower stall in the middle of Manila.

It's vital to remember that the huge majority of the smaller entrepreneurs live below or near the poverty level. Microcredit works because the borrowers in most of the plans do their banking as part of a group of peers of anywhere from 30 to 50 people. The banking now open to them means they apply for their loans, must set aside a percentage of the loan money for personal savings, and must pay interest on the loan. The group has authority to approve loan applications. Through its elected board it keeps tabs on the individual's repayments. It works with loan officers who carefully follow every transaction and know the strengths and troubles of each borrower.

Essentially, it's a family council whose members are related not by genes but by a common resolve to dig themselves and their families out of poverty.

The individuals in that group can't get a loan from a commercial bank. They don't have collateral, no matter how small the loan is. But in microcredit, the group becomes the collateral, guaranteeing repayment of the individual loan if Borrower X gets sick or falls behind. Microcredit works because these unsophisticated borrowers over the years have repaid those loans at an astonishing rate of more than 95 percent. The clients are unsophisticated because most of them are illiterate and start below or at the poverty level of an average income of $1 and $2 a day. Why is that performance remarkable? Consider that commercial banks around the world can't match that repayment rate on the loans they make.

Those loans have been repaid faithfully because nearly 90 percent of the borrowers are women, whose first and last commitment is to their families, their children. And that's where the bulk of the income from microcredit goes. Their stories are creating a new frontier of life in Africa and elsewhere. It dramatizes what is possible when the human will and ingenuity are joined by the good will and partnership of new friends thousands of miles away—the donors. These are people who understand the drive for dignity and education that fuels the ancient tradition of the entrepreneur.

So Susan Wilkes and I went on a different kind of exploration. For me, it was unlike the mountain climbing, trekking and camera safari expeditions I'd led for 20 years in the Himalayas and Africa; for her, it was unlike her work in developing countries and international outreach that had taken her to Bhutan, the Middle East, and Africa years before. We were married in 2001. The goals we shared in our social commitments came together in the belief that the poor in the developing countries had the same right to dream as we do, and that the same ambitions and yearnings that drive our lives stir in theirs. What is different is opportunity. Susan had been involved for years in nonprofit work and the management of family foundations. I had been a newspaper columnist and an organizer of international travel. The potential, the actual performance, of the microcredit movement fascinated us.

This book is an attempt to widen the awareness of that potential among people of good will who might be drawn to its power to change lives. Our purpose in our recent explorations in Africa, South America, and elsewhere was to take a realistic look at microcredit, at what its advocates believe is the most reliable road yet to alleviate world poverty and to empower the voiceless. That belief is founded on the simple premise of microcredit: helping the poor help themselves. The money to get them started or to build that tiny business is not a gift; it's a loan. It has to be repaid. If it's repaid, at interest, the reward is another loan to carry them further up the stairway. The ultimate reward is a new life of self-respect and achievement.

Americans raised in the codes of self-reliance and the supremacy of free and private enterprise instinctively applaud the concept of microcredit in the poorer countries—when they learn about it. Apart from major financial institutions and nonprofit organizations, scores of American family foundations and individuals looking for deserving causes have made that discovery in recent years.

The people you'll meet in this book make a compelling case for microcredit. They include the real heroes of micro, those ambitious poor people who know they can run a little business, have been willing to take risks to prove it, and have pulled their families out of the quagmire of poverty. But they also include people of means in America and elsewhere who have recognized the magic of this idea and have given their support.

A year before in our travels in Africa, Susan and I visited some of those small enterprisers in South America and Egypt, as we did later in sub-Saharan Africa and the Far East. The cultures were different—the colors, tongues and faces. The gratification we read in the eyes of those people, however, was the same in every country and every village. They had found a way, modest but exhilarating, to express those ambitions, to shed the fears of poverty and to turn the light of hope on their years ahead.

Some day, many of them vowed, their children would go to college—in La Paz, in Kampala, in Nairobi.

We saw some of those children, on their way to college diplomas.

—*Jim Klobuchar*
February 2003

CHAPTER ONE

The Greening of Barefoot Capitalism

This morning in Africa, in Bangladesh, Bolivia, and around the world—

Millions of people who were once abandoned as helpless losers in the jungles of poverty woke up to better lives.

There was food for their children to eat, where in the months or years before they scavenged garbage heaps in the alley or starved.

There were clothes for their children to wear, where in the months or years before they dressed in sacks or rags or stood naked.

There was money for the medicine their families needed to survive.

If their children were older, there was money for school.

For thousands of these people, almost miraculously, there was money in the bank; for some of them, these savings could now be used to send their older children to the university. They could study to be lawyers and engineers.

That was unimaginable a few years before. Poverty is not a fertile ground for fairy tales. But this is no empty dream.

The vast majority of these once most-depressed of the poor are women. They are women who have emerged from despair to find fulfillment and self-respect for themselves and their families.

What they have discovered for themselves and their families is an entirely new life that for the first time gives them choices. It is a new life in which they can walk confidently and live decently, can plan for the future and make a difference in their neighborhood or community.

No super government produced this extraordinary change in so many lives, nor was it the orchestration of some global Santa Claus movement.

For almost all of these people it began with a loan of less than $100.

It was a loan and not a gift. If the loan with interest could be repaid within four or five months, another loan would follow. And it followed almost invariably, because the record of repayment of those loans became astonishing—better than 95 percent in most countries over the last 30 years.

A loan of less than $100 placed in the hands of poor people of ambition, in societies as diverse as the Philippines, India, Uganda, Mexico, Bangladesh, India, Russia, Honduras, and dozens more, has since the 1970s changed the lives of hundreds of million people. The figures reflecting its impact today are extraordinary evidence of its power to transform. More than 2,000 microfinance institutions are delivering loans to nearly 40 million small-enterprise clients. Including members of their families, that multiplies to nearly 150 million people benefiting. Directly. Today.

None of this is the product of crafty bookkeeping, of smoke and mirrors accounting. It's called microcredit. If that doesn't sound particularly glamorous, try another: microfinance. That may not ring any gongs of immediate recognition, either. But it's worldwide, it's been happening for 30 years, and it's growing.

The downside is that it has not reached nearly a billion more people who are still mired in the deepest traps of poverty. For a moment consider the word "poverty." We use it incessantly because it is convenient and truthful, but we use it so often that the word alone can anesthetize us from the raw ugliness of what it means. Poverty means more than being poor. It means pain. It means humiliation. It means the indescribable agony of watching one's child die of starvation. It means, in the chilling words of Muhammad Yunus, "living like an animal."

Why should this matter to Americans, who can think of a lot of grief closer to home?

It matters to us more urgently today than it ever has before, quite apart from what that picture of hungry millions stirs in us as human beings. Poverty breeds a hopelessness that not only deadens the lives of millions of its victims, but can and does fuel resentments and hatreds that foster terror against the most advanced nations, beginning with the United States.

It's not only hunger that builds this rising anger and resentment. It's the misery of living in shacks and on garbage piles with nowhere to relieve themselves and no place to escape the brutal sun or the endless cold. What hurts more is the sense of abandonment, being ignored, ostracized by a world where people eat three meals a day, sleep in beds, and send their children to school.

Is America to blame for the refusal of the Islamic and Arab cultures of the Middle East to recognize the twenty-first or even the eighteenth century, for its hostility to the challenges and then the fruits of modernity? No, it isn't. It is not to blame for the epidemics or the civil wars or the self-perpetuating dictators and generals who have looted their own people.

But the reality of America in the early twenty-first century is that we have never felt more vulnerable. This is true at a time when we are the most powerful and wealthiest nation on earth, capable of building an undeclared empire in which our allies are now virtually vassals and doorkeepers. It is true at a time when we can drop the American flag almost anywhere on earth and say "boys, we're going to train here for the next war, and we promise not to stay for more than four or five years while we get combat-ready." America is that strong. Armies and economic competitors can't lay a glove on the United States. But self-constructed and lunatic angels of God with their suicide assaults and home-made bombs have persuaded the government of the United States to turn itself inside out, forcing massive reorganizations and some marginally dippy economics.

America is *not* responsible for the more than billion people living below the poverty line around the world. Yet it is capable of doing far more than it has at the government level to reduce that multitude of the starving. The architects of the World Trade attack were hardly poor. But the alienation that young men particularly feel in that lost world where they have no chance and no voice creates huge numbers of potential converts to terror. A handout from America isn't the answer. But giving them a chance to do what we do when we want to build a little business, to get a loan, can save them.

The irony here is that Americans privately, American family foundations, and some of America's corporate humanitarians remain as generous as they have been since the country began to prosper. And it is they who have made a crucial contribution to the movement called microcredit.

The microcredit phenomenon is today the single most compelling response to poverty in today's volatile world. Although it has rescued millions and thrust them into new and expanding lives, its formula is simple and totally transparent. What it doesn't have is enough money to reach the millions of the very poorest, to bring the system to them.

Why is it so simple and so easily functional? It comes down to making small loans available to poor people who can't put up the collateral in commercial banks for regular loans. But when they borrow in groups, their friends and neighbors in that group become their collateral. They set up or enlarge a tiny business—selling grain in the market, making clothes, catching fish, any one of a thousand little enterprises. They pay off the loan in four or five months, and get another. They can then make more clothes and catch more fish, and extra money comes into the house, and to the kids. If for some reason they can't make the repayment—illness or the needs of children, for example—their friends and neighbors in the group cover for them. The bond among them is that strong and personal.

Most American citizens in their own way work toward alleviating poverty around the world. They do it by contributing to a range of charities and church and other public and private collections.

Yet most American citizens are unaware of this most powerful and ongoing tool in the struggle to uplift the poor around the world. It unites the good will of people with access to money (foundations, corporations, individuals, and nonprofit agencies) with the capitalist instinct that stirs in most people regardless of their condition of life.

It is based on a remarkable discovery made by people who nourish this global movement with foundation or personal or non-profit money, or governmental funds. The discovery is this:

Poor people have yearnings like everybody else.

Poor people can be trusted like anybody else.

Poor people have energy and ambition like anybody else.

And nobody in these multitudes of the poor has the yearnings, energy, and ambition that mothers have.

What they haven't had and need is a chance to turn hope into something they can build. The movement of microcredit has now opened that door for them and brought in the fresh air of opportunity they've never had.

One of the popular adages of our time borrows its message from an ancient profundity. Give a man a fish and you feed him for a day. Teach him to fish and you feed him for a lifetime. It is the cornerstone of a hundred fund-raising campaigns. It contains truth and it is inspirational.

But the phenomenon of microcredit does much more.

It can feed families for a lifetime by empowering millions of small business people—once called peasants, once called peons—to build and expand their flower stalls, to raise pigs, to sell pots and pans and a thousand other things. That is a new and renewable source of food.

But it also teaches them how to budget their money, how to bank, how to keep books, how invest, how to bond with their neighbors and fellow microfinanciers to set their own rules of banking and lending, how to police their small market operations, and how to rescue a neighbor who misses a payment.

What it does, in short, is to transform that person into somebody larger than before, with wider horizons and a life of growing vitality and deeper self-respect and confidence.

A question: "Aren't millions living below our poverty line in America?" They are. "If microcredit is so marvelous in the more primitive economies of the world, why don't we see more of it in the United States?"

Microcredit has experienced isolated pockets of success in this country, but the numbers of people who have seen some benefit in it are infinitesimal alongside those in the developing countries. There are several reasons. The essence of microcredit's staying power in the poor countries is the stratospheric rate of repayment of its loans, in the 95 percent range. It can only achieve that level through the group or village banking method, where 20 to 50 people join in communal banking to create collateral. The concept is ingrained in many of the cultures of the poor countries. It is not part of the American culture with its homage to individualism. People who might want to risk taking a loan to build a small business in the United States normally have to shoulder that risk by themselves, and the money it takes to build or expand a small enterprise in America is proportionately much bigger than the kind of loans microcredit can comfortably deal with in Africa or South America.

Increasingly in recent years, microcredit borrowing by the poor elsewhere in the world has brought with it social services that are now recognized by its providers as a crucial part of the microcredit plan: education in disease prevention, family planning, and community support. Millions of children orphaned by AIDS are now being supported by foster parents who have been shored up with extra income from microcredit.

What is unfolding in scores of money-strapped countries around the world is a kind of mini-capitalism that the practical, hardheaded capitalist in the West can admire, and in fact, even envy. And what is emerging now is a link between the two. Despite Enron and the rest of the misbehaving corporate giants in America, despite an economic downtown in 2001 and the September 11 trauma, America's surge of prosperity in the last 10 or 12 years is without precedent. Thousands of Americans found themselves enjoying a personal wealth they could not have imagined, money into the millions. Those new riches confronted some of them with surprising dilemmas, not the least of which is "what do reasonable people do with all this money?"

They'll reserve a lot of it for the children, of course, and for their grandchildren. But after those commitments are made, what then? Making family heirlooms out of millions of dollars isn't necessarily in the best interests of the family, many have come to realize. So how much will they give to those who need it more, to institutions, to causes that are in struggle? The choices are endless. Some of those pragmatic American entrepreneurs now find a compelling case for shaving of a modest slice of their largesse and making it available to those ambitious poor people who know they can run a little business and, with it, pull their families out of the quagmire of poverty.

Julie Oswald and other members of her family had accepted that idea well before she and other members of her family arrived from Minneapolis at the airport in La Paz, Bolivia. The scene as their flight descended toward the runway was stunning. La Paz lay in a vast amphitheater carved in thin air nearly three miles above the sea and rimmed by some of the most spectacular snow mountains of the Andes. Julie Oswald also knew that despite the transcending beauty of the scene below, Bolivia was one of the poorest countries on earth.

Like most countries in what we now call the developing world or Global South (once the Third World or the Undeveloped Countries), Bolivia had suffered on the familiar rack of ancient tribal struggles, colonization, the illusions of liberation by revolutionary generals and religious hierarchies. It has been exploited by foreign corporations and richer societies and smothered by the rule of military juntas. It has lived with the promises of visionaries and genuine Samaritans, the illusions of land reform and guerrilla warfare against corrupt governments. Finally, Bolivia has been mired in even deeper poverty caused by the runaway technological superiority of richer lands.

So was Bolivia a hopeless case?

Julie Oswald's family didn't think so. Several years ago it had created a foundation that flowed from the wealth of the family patriarch, a creative and energetic one-man conglomerate, Charley Oswald, from Kansas; then Harvard; Owatonna, Minnesota; Minneapolis; Custer, South Dakota; Colorado; and a dozen other places. Charley was and is one of those corporate wizards, a man who creates winners wherever he goes. He built a family fortune, which came with a conscience. Beginning several years ago, the Oswalds have met annually to research human need in America and those parts of the world with which the family—the six brothers and sisters and Charley—have some familiarity. In this they had been encouraged by Sally Oswald, Charley's wife, who died in the 1990s. Out of these meetings materialized grants totaling several hundred thousand dollars annually.

Some of that money went to Bolivia. In the summer of 2001, Julie, Tom Oswald, Carolyn Oswald Workman, and Carolyn's two daughters flew to Bolivia to learn whether that money was a wistful gesture or meant something important that had or could change lives.

What they found changed their own lives.

The Oswalds were conscious in advance of the awesome mathematics of poverty in the world today, the nearly 2 billion people in the world living on less than $2 a day. That's almost a third of the world's people. Most of them can't find jobs. If they do, not many of those jobs provide a living wage.

So is a struggling dressmaker in La Paz or Manila or Dar es Salaam condemned to a grubbing, joyless obscurity without a hope of escape for herself or her children because she can't get a $75 loan from a commercial bank to buy more material?

The short form answer the Oswalds found in Bolivia is no.

The dressmaker can't put up the money or goods to guarantee the loan, and she doesn't want to get trapped into paying 400 percent interest to a loan shark. The Oswald family was in Bolivia in support of an option that exists for that dressmaker today. She can get that loan of $75 on her simple agreement to repay it with interest. The record showing that she *will* repay, backed by the credibility of her solidarity group, is unequivocal.

Microcredit grows under a mass of umbrella organizations, ranging from nonprofit institutions to family foundations like the Oswald's, government agencies, banks, non-government organizations, humanitarian groups, and individuals. They provide the seed money for loan management organizations that have affiliates or partners around the world, institutions that act as the banks for microcredit borrowers. The borrowers are those millions of small entrepreneurs like the dressmaker. The umbrella groups and their partners in the poor countries are not misty-eyed handholders. Almost all of them answer to bedrock principles of sound economics: accountability, sustainability, and more. They include international heavy hitters like Deutsche Bank, the Calvert Foundation, Citigroup, the Rockefellers, and the Fords.

The money they commit to microcredit is not charitable giving. Microcredit, they insist, has to pay its own way. That means the borrowers, although poor, have to pay enough interest to keep the system going and building. It has to be, in other words, sustainable. This means it has to be self-sufficient, not propped up indefinitely by donations. It has to insulate itself against bad times and against competition that has eventually come from the commercial bankers themselves—who marvel at that high rate of loan repayments by the poor.

And where does the donated money go? The affiliates, on the ground, develop a pool of money from the donors. Through local banks and networks of the borrowers themselves, they make loans to small enterprisers who typically form solidarity groups of 30 to 50 people. They come to their meetings with their curled rupees or shillings in hand, the modest cash that will meet their repayment deadlines for the week or the month. But they come with something else—their will and longing to make something better for themselves and their families. Do you want to call that a vision? Why not? Visions are not confined to saints and conglomerate CEOs. When you come from a rich country like the United States—where often we'll do some casual bitching about the innate malice of the freeway traffic jam—the sight of poor people lifting themselves out of the dead end of their lives can fill you with humility and respect.

The generally accepted pioneer of modern microcredit is Muhammad Yunus, an economist with a huge canvas of ideas for giving the poor access to capital. The ultimate monument to his trail blazing, the Grameen Bank in Bangladesh, became the archetype of microcredit lending around the world. While Yunus began giving microcredit a global spread in the 1970s, the organization ACCION in South America had already evolved as one of the major providers in international microcredit.

ACCION was founded 40 years ago by a idealistic law student and amateur tennis player named Joseph Blatchford, who was appalled and moved by the conditions on which people lived in many of the Latin American countries where his tennis tour trouped. Today it is world-wide in its reach and not bashful about what its goals and missions are. "It is not enough to help 1,000 or even 100,000 individuals," ACCION will tell you today. "Our goal is to bring microlending to millions of people, enough to truly change this (South American) hemisphere and, ultimately, the world. We know there will never be enough (charitable) donations to do this. That's why ACCION has created an anti-poverty strategy that is permanent and self-sustaining."

And how is that achieved?

ACCION works with its hundreds of affiliate networks and with its major banking partners (of which Banco Sol in Bolivia is the flagship) to grow its borrowers' interest payments and donor contributions and investments. Shaped largely by the Otero family, ACCION expanded in great bounds and now deals in hundreds of millions of dollars and can provide its own guarantees to its patrons. And because it does, it can provide the due diligence that any responsible financial institution needs to exert, although its tens of thousands of clients often receive loans of less than $100 and have no experience in banking. But they *do* have to learn bookkeeping. They are seamstresses, pot makers, bakers, growers, flower peddlers—whatever has a market. They are clients because they repaid their first loan at interest rates comparable to the commercial bank rates. But Banco Sol is their bank. It gave them the loan, and they are loyal to it.

The trust works two ways. The low-income borrowers earned a second loan, and then a third, and now they are regulars. They are making money, and so is the bank. Somewhere down the road if they need $3,000 to start a shop, that money is very likely going to be available. A credit officer will visit his or her clients once a week, ledgers in hand. The credit officer will thread through the chaotically merry market downtown in the city of Cochabamba in the Bolivian Andes.

The Oswald family on its visit to the site of some of its donations, including ACCION's network, walks with him under the blistering sun. It becomes a sweaty, absorbing field trip. Lesson one for Carolyn, Julie, Tom, and the teenagers: philanthropy can be hugely revealing about the world they live in, and it can be about the joy of discovery as well as the serious business of generosity. One of their discoveries is the depth and immediacy of the connection they feel with the people in need to whom they have committed themselves. It's an easy intimacy and friendship they hadn't expected. The credit officer strides past the mountains of grain and gourds and fruit in first three tiers of the market and then comes to the musical instruments. It is a whole forest of musical instruments, lorded over by the guitars and charangos and in the middle of it is Martha Lopez Arnez, 48. She is a bright woman of bountiful physique, racking up another sale of a charango that is lacquered handsomely and ready for somebody's fiesta.

She is one of Banco Sol's customers and the credit officer doesn't have to ask many questions. She knows the credit business. It rescued her from the pits five years ago. Tom Oswald asks her how she did it. She says her husband makes charangos—string instruments similar to guitars—but nobody would lend her money to go into the market with them. She wanted the money to buy a house larger than their old one, which was too small for the family. Banco Sol lent her $100, with which she and her husband bought three different kinds of wood to make the charangos. Customers liked them. She got more loans, then finally a bonanza of $3,000 to shoot for a bigtime splash in the charango market. They made it. And the children, Tom asked?

They fared pretty well, for the family was knit together with love, charango strings, and microcredit. One of the children is an auditor. Another is studying law. Another is finishing in psychology this year. And when they started, there was no money in the house and no college in sight.

You're obviously not going to eradicate poverty in the world by doling out $75 loans to people who will repay those loans, but may have to grub along all of their lives barely staying afloat financially. This means microcredit has to be a lot more than banking gimmickry to presume to make major sociological differences in the world. It can't subsist making those tiny and touching loans. En masse, they're a costly banking practice.

So the microcredit institution has to make enough money to afford writing those little loans, which means it has to get into the thick of leveraging important capital and often doing, in fact, some big league banking of its own. And while it's doing that, the voices of conscience in the microcredit movement are saying, "Don't forget the poorest of the poor. If you do, you betray the only important charter you have."

We need to look at those dilemmas, and we need to look at something else. The microcredit movement has to deal with some criticism. It has trouble reaching the very poorest who live beyond the roads, beyond phones and electricity. When it gets too big it can have trouble servicing all those small loans. The worst curses of the poor, critics say, are lack of adequate medical care, lack of quality education, lack of education at all, and the poor to non-existent welfare systems in the backward countries in which they live. Some argue that microcredit isn't doing enough to solve that. Watching some of the success of microcredit, they say, can persuade financially strapped governments in those countries to ignore their own responsibilities to the poor.

There is truth in some of that, but also a quibble. More microcredit operations each year are insisting on bringing education and social service to the table as part of the weekly group meetings. No social or economic innovation is spared some discernible down-side. Microcredit hasn't revealed any gaping downside that would offset the new vitality and hope and dignity—life itself—that it has brought to millions. The dressmaker who couldn't get a conventional loan, who refused to deal with the loan shark, is real. She's not rich today. But she's making more dresses, bringing more money into her home, and feeding her kids because she asked for and received that first loan. And now her world is different. She has friends she meets each week.

And her fears are gone because she is no longer alone.

CHAPTER 2

When Women Decide to be Unstoppable

The sight of women being forced to dress in their uniform of submission, the head-to-toe burqa decreed by the Taliban in Afghanistan, left millions of television watchers appalled. This, after all, was the twenty-first century.

But while they were being offended and angered, the American television audiences might well have asked themselves a question. When was it that women in America, that most enlightened of democracies, received the most fundamental of all rights of citizenship—the right to vote?

And the answer, of course, is well into the twentieth century. The struggle of women to gain the same rights, power, and basic dignity as men is as old as civilization itself. That struggle for equality clearly has made significant headway for women in the prosperous West in the last 100 years. It has made those advances in the courtroom, the legislative hearing rooms, the bedroom and the corporate boardrooms. But the condition of women in most of the world—the Middle East, Africa, great sweeps of Asia, and in Latin America—is almost as benighted today as it was in the age of the cave dwellers.

If a social evangelist had a choice of picking one tool, one movement with the goal of emancipating the poorest women on earth, the microcredit phenomenon wins without serious competition. And why are the poorest so important? Because women at the lowest end of the world's economic and social spectrum are the most repressed, the truly voiceless, the truly powerless. They are also the most numerous, into the hundreds of millions, and they cut across almost all of the ethnic, religious, and cultural roadmaps. And because they are the mothers of the poor, they are the only true salvation of the multitudes of children who are doomed without hope unless their families can produce enough income to protect their health, to feed them adequately, and to give them a fighting chance to learn in school.

Microcredit has opened that door for millions of women and therefore for their families. And why is that good news for America and the rest of the developed world?

It means suffering, ignorance, and hunger around the world have been reduced. For anybody of conscience and the normal compassion, that might be enough. But it means more. It means we have cut into that enormous gulf between those who live comfortably and in relative luxury and those who have to claw and grasp and hunt for scraps just to stay alive. It means that relieving poverty, at least in modest increments, makes this a better and safer world. It is a safer world because poverty ignored eventually will explode into violence and even into genocide. And if it does, it's small consolation to tell ourselves, "we're not to blame. We worked hard and deserve the life we have." We undoubtedly do. But the experience of microcredit, which is fundamentally supported and expanded by the industrial West, tells us how far enlightened (and not necessarily charitable) Samaritanism can go in liberating the disadvantaged. Remember, those are loans, not gifts.

Shift the television camera now from Afghanistan to East Africa. The Maasai culture in Africa, like the Maasai warrior of decades ago and the herdsman of today, is lean and hard. The Maasai adolescents still undergo excruciating circumcision rites, both boys and girls. The surmounting code for the males is to be fearless. Facing a lion, they are. Facing their women, they have been historically brutal.

They have abused and suppressed their women for centuries. It is part of traditional behavior. But today across Africa, the rank sexism of those cultures is changing, visibly and in some places dramatically, as it is in many of the world's developing countries that were once called primitive.

Sometimes it helps to put a face to a landmark change in how a once-abused people are treated. In the African savannah where the Maasai live, the face is that of a buoyant and hefty Maasai woman named Sinyati Lebene, a 61-year-old mother of six with songs on her lips, a bountiful torso, and eyes that dance like fireflies. For a collar she wears a bright beaded shanga, the familiar Maasai necklace that Sinyati displays both as an ornament and kind of billboard for her business. For years she has been wife number one of a Maasai cattle owner whose menage grew to four wives. At one time, he would beat her routinely when she asked him for money. He doesn't now. She earns her own money and makes most of the decisions that affect her life.

"It was never that way before," she said, "It started to change when I joined the other women. They told me about credit. They said I could repay the money I borrowed. It was the biggest thing I've done in my life."

Hers was a declaration that might serve as the mantra for millions of women around the world. Their lives changed when the doors swung open for them at the neighborhood bank. It was not the conventional bank as westerners understand banks. What opened to women was the wonder of simple credit—a wonder because until 25 or 30 years ago, poor women approaching a bank cashier's window in Tanzania or Bolivia or India would have been rousted off the premises by uniformed guards. They were lucky to escape arrest as vagrants. Poor people, especially poor women, had no collateral. With no banking history, with little or no education, with practically nothing to their names, they were an impossible credit risk.

Muhammad Yunus didn't think so. Yunus is the economist whose education spans both Asia and America and who, in the 1970s, introduced the principle of microcredit in his native Bangladesh. Because the poor had nothing to guarantee repayment, Yunus and pioneers like him created a way. The borrowers, 90 percent of them women, formed a credit group, a partnership of the poor. Together they could put up enough money to bail out any member who fell short in his or her payments. The $50 to $100 loans they took would come due in four to six months at something like 1 percent a week in interest. They also had to put down 5 percent in savings. For them it was a load. But the moral power of the group made it manageable. The seed money didn't blow in from the snows of Kilimanjaro. It came from nonprofits and foreign governments that funded the Maasai women's group originally. The equation is this: Donors initially provide the pool for loans and operations, but the microcredit institution itself, made up of all its members, will some day be big enough and disciplined enough to make it without donors. It will have to be. Microcredit makes poor people bankable, and their bank—the source of their loans—can't be subsidized indefinitely.

This is how the poor are digging themselves out of the dumping grounds of society around much of the world. And yet the visitor to Africa is mildly astonished to hear a Sinyati Lebene, the rollicking Maasai grandmother, embracing a technical, impersonal buzz word like "microcredit" as though it were a spiritual epiphany in her life.

But it has been something close to that for Sinyati and for millions of other women who now find themselves empowered in ways they would not have foreseen only a few years ago. To understand why microcredit has been so crucial for impoverished and struggling women of the world, it might be instructive to take the visions of independence held by American women and compare them with those of women in the poor countries. American women demanded and fought for open doors that would give them access to broader options and choices in their lives, to equality in the workplace, control over their bodies, and greater access to the hierarchies of power. Much of this came down to access to money and mobility. Much of it has been achieved.

In the poor countries, it came down to liberation from the psychological prisons of male domination and of the actual peonage of women. The world's money brokers often sneer at the poor as dumb and lazy people without a clue about how to make it in the world. The truth is that most of the world's poor people *aren't* dumb or lazy or without dreams or creativity. They are simply poor, most of them born that way. And when the opportunities of microcredit began to open, the lenders quickly saw that the most reliable borrowers were likely to be women. Why? When women turned those small loans into more dresses or soap to sell or used it to build larger handicraft kiosks, the first beneficiaries of that new money invariably would be their children's health and education. There is no greater incentive for a woman. So they were almost a cinch to repay the loan.

It has worked out that way in millions of families.

The head of one of the world's major players among microfinance institution is Nancy Barry, a mover and something of an all-purpose dynamo in the field of emancipating the poor. In the 1989 she left a position with the World Bank, where she was responsible for 40 percent of that institution's entire portfolio, to become president of Women's World Banking (WWB). Somebody asked her why she would step away from so prestigious a role to run a non-government agency with four employees.

She replied, "I believed then and I believe now that the biggest changes in uplifting the poor and especially poor women are going to happen through smaller institutions. We can be an aggressive and creative. In fact, we have to be. The key is in working with affiliates that have developed strong and reliable leadership in the poor countries. Look, to make headway, these women have to be as hard as nails.

There's the story about a high official of the central bank who went out to meet hundreds of angry women in one of the Far East countries. They wanted better access. They waved fingers at him and demanded to know whether he helped his wife in the kitchen."

The guy was overmatched, clearly. He left the scene in disarray but with some fresh ideas about how to provide credit for angry women. It is a matter of record that the leader of the women who confronted the big shot banker eventually organized a cooperative of more than 100,000 basically illiterate women whose leaders insisted on an inviolable creed: "Make sure they repay the loans."

"If commercial banks had that philosophy," Nancy Barry said, "there'd be a lot less trouble in banking today.

"What's emerged in the years since Yunus got microcredit rolling is that women in the poor countries have become an undeniable force. They are not helpless. They are powerful. Out of the Bangladesh model and its later variations came successful banking systems and how to work with the poor. Nobody has to look at microfinance for poor women as some kind of charming, cute poodle of world corporate life. The truth is that it works better than corporate finance. It works in good times, but particularly in bad times. It builds itself on the shoulders of people like the woman in the Dominican Republic who started out as a garment factory worker when she was 13. She dreamed then of some day having a white wedding gown. So she took out a micro loan. She started out with one sewing machine, and in a few years she was running a factory that subcontracted to self-employed women. And later she stood up at a microcredit conference and shouted, 'If I can do it, anybody can.' Women cheered."

But she brought down the house when she raised her arm and shouted again, "If women don't do it (help other women), *nobody* will."

Are there risks that go beyond meeting the loan, beyond potential resentful glares both from males and from village women willing to accept traditional roles for women?

There are. A woman who is a member of a WWB affiliate in Colombia reported to a hushed audience not long ago, "Drug gangs murdered 23 of our clients in their place of business."

Her organization is still operating.

Barry was asked another question: "In the historic, if uneven, advance of women (remembering the scenes of hooded women still current in 2002) how important is microcredit?"

She said, "It's not a panacea. It doesn't change the world over-night. But this, to me, is the most important lever. It's more important than the vote. What must come first is empowerment, financially and socially. It can give women, and by extension their families, control over their lives, or certainly that possibility. That gives women a fundamentally different attitude toward the future. It brings not only dignity, but hope, and now an even stronger motivation. The reasons it's working that way are clear. Before microfinance, families didn't think seriously about educating girls. But because women now are serious about that, and because they're always serious about the health of their children, they're repaying those loans, and the ranks of women now building their lives and their family's lives with microcredit keep growing."

It's not all fairy tale stuff. There's some evidence that maintaining a loan by working away from home allows some women less time with their children, to the detriment of the children. There's also evidence that some husbands will steal loan money or build resentments over the woman's changing role.

Yet this evidence seems strongly outweighed by the microcredit ledgers around the world revealing the millions of women who are recycling their loans and bringing more money into the family and therefore into their communities.

A fascinating part of this social evolution, still invisible to much of the gentrified world, is that it doesn't reveal itself to be a movement of some vast and hulking herd. The gift of microcredit is that it has allowed each woman the discovery of another self—her individualism. And from the ranks of the once-marginalized women of Africa have emerged managers and executives like Eva Mukasa, the general man-ager of the Uganda Women's Finance Trust Fund, an affiliate of Women's World Banking. Here is a breezy and confident executive with her hair smartly combed back, vaguely amused eyes when she is discussing big banking numbers, and an MBA in her portfolio. She has thousands of clients, some of them now capable of managing loans of more than $1,000. But it is the poorest of those clients who get her most earnest attention. She has seen poverty much of her life. She has the brains, the training, and the spine to bring poor women into her offices, which Ugandans now call "The Women's Bank." If they are first timers, they are frightened and overwhelmed. Eva tells them they can make it and shows them how. And most of them make it.

But if the clients of microcredit prize that emergence of their undiscovered identities, the other self of the Maasai woman in Tanzania, Sinyati Lebene, is a rollicking and impressive package. She speaks Maasai and Kiswahili, but it was a chore for the interpreter to get all of the syllables out, because Sinyate was sailing on a monologue of gratitude when we overtook her.

She was asked about those horror images of women in a polygamous Maasai household getting up before the sun, hauling water, building the fire, cooking in the smoke-filled huts, feeding, milking, and doing all of the drudgery.

She shrugged. "Sure. I get up early. It's the way we live. I get the water and milk the cows and make the meal and dress the children. I'm the number one wife. People say that must give some privileges. Not much. My husband's second wife died. One of my children was killed in an accident. I had six others, and I help take care of the eight children of the second wife. I don't know what privileges[they're talking about]. When a second wife comes in she gets some of the things the first wife owns, and maybe a cow or two.

"But when I found out about this credit group (Women Empowerment and Development Agency Company, WEDAC), I finally saw a way I could do some of the things I wanted to do. I could be my own person.

"I've had five loans in five years," she said. "Do you want to know something?"

I said I wouldn't tell a soul.

"I love my life. Nobody knew how this was going to work because in the Maasai, the men are in control. But the elders had these meetings and they said, okay, go ahead and see what happens."

What happened was that Martha Umbulla, who is the godmother of WEDAC, started rounding up her troops in a four-wheel drive commissioned by the McKnight Foundation in Minnesota. Her clients lived miles apart, in boma settlements or in villages. Martha wheeled around the Maasai savannah, dodging a lion here and there, to make sure she got maximum attendance at the meetings. Weekly meetings are critical for village banking groups because the borrowers get training there in bookkeeping, make their payments, and apply for new loans. There's one more critical component in those meetings. Bishop Thomas Laizer of the Evangelical Lutheran Church in Arusha talks about it with emotion.

"It's important that these women have a forum," he said. "Look, I grew up in a Maasai house. The word of the tribal leaders was final. Women weren't heard from. There's no question that Maasai women have suffered historically. I'm on the board of WEDAC because I believe in what it can do in building the lives of women and expanding the lives of their children and their communities. This is not just about loans and credit. This is about life. The women are a tremendous asset that has been ignored. These were people who have had to walk eight miles every day to get water and walk back again. And now with the money they make in these small enterprises, they can help build a system where water is delivered to their houses, and they can pay for it. In this forum they can talk to other women about health, about emotional problems, about choices. They can make decisions individually and as a group. They can listen to health experts telling them how to protect themselves from HIV infection, and they can hear this same expert tell them they have a right to say 'no.'"

But is this last an illusion?

"He's right," Martha Umbulla said. "For the first time in their lives, these women are experiencing the right to make decisions on their own because now they have their own assets and they don't have to depend solely on male decisions. They now bring up family planning. They've learned about group support. And they know how to handle interest and savings."

And how does all that translate for the effervescent Sinyati Lebene? "I started by making collars with beads and selling them, then I went to buying and selling food. I still do a big business making *loshoro*. Hey, do you know what that is? You boil maize overnight and cool it the next day and mix it with sour milk. It's like mush, like yogurt, and everybody loves it. You ought to try it."

Right.

She's fundamentally unstoppable, Sinyati. In later years she moved into livestock, buying a few cows and goats and fattening them, reselling at a 30 percent profit. With four other women she went into a partnership to buy seed and share the profits from the plots of ground that each of them owned. One of those women was her husband's third wife. Another was the daughter of the fourth wife.

It's a different kind of society, this.

"People ask, are you jealous of the other wives?" Sinyati said. "With me, no. The others share in some of the things I bring home.

Life has changed. I said my husband doesn't beat me anymore. That's the way life was then. I started doing my own work and making my own money. He thought that was all right. He doesn't take any of my money, although some Maasai men do. My husband doesn't care now when I come home, because he knows I've got my own things to do. When my oldest boy was killed in the accident, I couldn't pay my loan on time because the time was so bad for me. My husband sold one of his cows to pay it for me. This might sound different to you, but he's a good man and I love him. And I love my life now. I never thought I'd say that."

She grabbed the arms of her two friends in the small meeting hall and sang her way out into the yard, making up the words of her chants as she sang.

The women in the life of Wanjiku Kironyo of Nairobi, Kenya, are not so joyful. Wanjiku is a sociology professor who was appalled to learn about the lives of young women in the slums Nairobi. Many of them are girls from the farm country who give their early years to cooking and caring for males in the family. In their cultures, most of these girls can't inherit land. When they reach the teen years, they're no longer welcome at home. Without schooling or skills, with no life left for them in their villages, they will head for a city like Nairobi, trying to survive. A girl may find work as a housemaid in a rich home. More often than not, Wanjiku found, the girl is used sexually by the man of the house, gets pregnant and is tossed out. She becomes a bargirl and the contract is clear: she's expected to boost sales by offering her body to customers.

She becomes pregnant again and loses her job. She now has two children and no income. What's left is prostitution or selling alcohol illegally. The police arrest her. She does six months in prison because there is no one to make bail for her. She has nothing to pawn. She returns to the street and finds herself back in jail. The cycle goes on. This is a life in ruin, but more than one life. There are the children, adrift. And what about the hundreds of women trying to escape abusive marriages, unable to go home because their families have paid a dowry to the husband? Their cycles are the same as those of the farm girls.

Multiply their lives by thousands, because many of these women have up to 8 or 12 children. It gets worse and uglier. Sometimes a 14-year-old girl is having her first child while her mother is having her seventh. If the child has a mental disorder with which the mother cannot cope, the child will slowly starve to death.

Wanjiku responded by organizing the Maji Mazuri Center in Nairobi, to which she now devotes a major part of her professional life. It has been a wrenching but vital rescue mission for scores of these battered and luckless women. What's saving them is not only the professional care of trained health workers but the redemptive power of microcredit. In groups of 18 to 20 the women receive small loans from the center, set up tiny businesses and repay their loans at a nearby post bank. "They learn," Wanjiku said, "to sell vegetables instead of their bodies. They learn that there are people they can trust, people who care for them. They become role models for their daughters. They learn about family planning and how to work together and how to pool their resources. They talk openly about AIDS and learn how to prevent it." And what started them back into the clean air of personal dignity was trust in somebody who cared, and knowing that they themselves could now be trusted.

The money they borrow and repay may be trivial by western standards. But it is the world and new life for women once outcast and abandoned.

CHAPTER 3

The Forgotten Wisdom of Harry Truman

In the hours immediately after the attack of September 11, 2001, the shock and anger engulfing America from ocean to ocean fused its diverse faces and voices into a solidarity of grief and purpose the country had never known outside of World War II.

The uneasiness came later and has not disappeared. We now face an unknown we have never experienced. Americans have become targets of global guerrilla warfare and probably will be for the rest of their lives. There is no way to predict where the next attack will come, and in spite of toughened homeland security and the might of the country's military here and overseas, it could come not only in America, but anywhere in the world where Americans or American interests are exposed.

The level of risk at the hands of people deranged by hatred can't be calibrated. It may be remote, but the threat is there. So the thought of a new outbreak of terror in America lingers in our minds and recurs even in the most casual conversations. Therefore, it was common for Americans to tell each other in the aftermath of 9/11 that "nothing will ever be the same."

But some things didn't change. They may have to change soon, if America is to recover the security it felt before 9/11.

This didn't change:

- In the year 2001, like the year before and the year before that, more than 10 million children died from diseases that could have been prevented with minimal care.

- Millions of others, adults and children, died of starvation.

- In the year 2001, like the year before and the year before that, more than 100 million children of primary school age were not in school because there was no school where they lived or because their parents didn't have money to keep them in school.

• In the year 2001, nearly two billion people in the world were economic outcasts, without access to the most simple, most fundamental of financial services, locked into poverty without a hope of escape.

Public hearings on world poverty are standard fare in the industrial and more prosperous countries. A typical scenario goes like this:

Somebody recites the numbers, and they are horrendous. Millions starving, millions doomed by disease that could be treated with a few dollars in America. The panelists—most of them knowledgeable people of good will— shrug and sigh and sound earnest. In the end they admit being stumped about how to provide meaningful relief to starving people. Some wars can be stopped. Poverty can't, they say, at least not soon enough to save millions from dying or living helpless lives.

In the ensuing Q and A, a voice in the audience asks a question like this: "Aren't poverty and the huge disparity in living conditions and health service around the world two of the main causes of war and violence? Aren't those conditions being mined by terrorists and political revolutionaries, who draw on the futility and emotional isolation that fester in poverty?"

A panelist nods and says yes, that's a danger. He quickly follows with a question for the questioner:"Do you have something better than what we've been trying?"

The question meant "something better than giving away money and food and know-how."

But there are multitudes of women around the world who know of another route and who have entered a new world of their own because of it. Ironically, it is a scheme that should rev-up the ideological glands of the most hardrock conservative who has gone through a lifetime snarling at marshmallow idealists bent on saving the world. You don't have to be an evangelist wading through the jungle to know that for millions of people today, microcredit is a better way.

When they get a close look at the figures, commercial bankers are likely to agree. How many commercial banks get a 95 percent repayment on their small loans? And the truth about those millions of borrowers in microcredit in the poor countries is that every one of them is capitalist.

It doesn't matter that some of them live in socialist countries, some of them under military dictatorships and some of them in countries that have no discernible government—in fact no discernible country. For human ambition there are no international borders and no passport requirements. It doesn't matter that millions of clients of microcredit are Islamic, that some are Africans, some Arabs, some Latin Americans or that thousands live in and are citizens of the United States of America. Millions are Christian, millions Hindu, some are atheists and more can't tell you where they are spiritually because they—like many with money to burn—haven't figured it out. It doesn't matter that you'll find dirt under the fingernails of most of these capitalists and no school degrees after their names.

What you find is an obsession to make it. What you find further for millions of them is an absolute, life-or-death *need* to make it. They are all in business. Never mind that those businesses don't often appear in the lead stories in the Wall Street Journal or the Economist. To get there or to stay there these people had to put up interest for a loan, as much as 30 percent interest. It was the best their sympathetic lenders could come up with and still keep the microbank open. Yet the vast majority of these people have met the terms of their loan. It was either that or fall back into the muck and facelessness of poverty.

Before we look at how microcredit has taken hold, we need to know why it has emerged as a promising and potentially vital response to terror.

The Global Greengrants Fund can tell you. It exists to strengthen small environmental movements around the world. As part of this work it gives you a look at the staggering proportions of where the wealth is in the world today. Imagine a global village of 100 people, who will represent how the world's population and wealth are distributed.

These people would include 58 Asians; 15 Europeans; 14 from North, Central, and South America; and 12 from Africa. Thirty would be Caucasian and 70 non-white. Thirty would be Christian and 70 non-Christian. One-third of these people would be children.

Of all the income available, 20 people would get 75 percent, and 20 would get only 2 percent.

Six people, or six percent of the entire global population, would control 50 percent of the global wealth.

All six of those would be U.S. citizens.

The three richest people in the world have assets that exceed the combined gross national products of 48 countries.

Of all the global goods and services, the richest one-fifth consumes 86 percent. The poorest fifth consumes 1.3 percent. In Africa, the average house consumes 20 percent less today than it did in 1975.

Those figures, while recent, are somewhat dated even today, and the lopsided scale is even worse.

Should we feel guilty in America about all that? A more suitable reaction, probably, is to be appalled, and after that, to feel a rising anxiety.

Hungry, destitute, and powerless people were often left in that condition because international politics or their primitive cultures shut them out of the fruits available to luckier or more aggressive or better educated people. Or they were helpless to find their way out of the morass created by their self-indulgent or religiously fanatical potentates. It is axiomatic that sooner or later many of these people, smothered in powerlessness and seemingly ignored by the world, eventually find a way to express their bitterness and envy. Some of them do this by turning to revolutionary political movements, or sometimes by supporting mindless violence.

Has American public policy made a contribution to this troublesome state of the world?

It has, because in 50 years we have systematically devalued the power of our good will, slashed our assistance to people and nations in need, and increasingly politicized our acts of cooperation or generosity by telling people "either you're with us or you're against us." It is a slogan with at least one virtue: It leaves no doubt about our intentions. But it also leaves much of the world wondering whether we want its cooperation or submission.

There's a fair proposition and question here. We have gained enormously in power and influence since the end of World War II. And despite the turn of the century economic slump we have produced vast new wealth. So what have we really lost by shrinking our government aid to struggling people?

The former director of the major U.S. assistance program, USAID, suggests some answers to that question.

J. Brian Atwood ran the program in the Clinton administration, by which time USAID's allocation of funds had been sliced to the bone by a succession of presidential administrations, Republican and Democratic. In late 2002, he became head of the Humphrey Institute of Public Affairs in Minneapolis, an organization that explores today's world of human need, global politics and global economics. At the time of USAID's organization (originally Harry Truman's Point 4 of the massive rebuilding of shattered countries after World War II) America had begun assigning 15 percent of its entire budget to foreign aid. That figure represented nearly 100 percent of the world's outlay to help poor and battered countries. Today the U.S. share is down to 15 percent and the USAID resources represent a woefully shriveled one-half of 1 percent of the entire U.S. budget.

In a talk before members of the Minnesota International Center in the fall of 2002, Atwood looked back at what he saw as results of America's aid program of 50 years ago:

"We saved millions of children by assuring that they received inoculations against childhood diseases and oral rehydration therapy (and) thus cut the infant mortality rate in half.

"We made clean water available to millions . . .

"We introduced family planning programs that enabled the poor to avoid unwanted pregnancies and to space their children so they could provide health care and education for them . . .

"We helped governments to develop environmental protection plans (and) we financed micro-credit facilities to offer help to those who wanted to start small businesses . . .

"In short, we transformed people's lives, we won the Cold War, and we produced a new democratic revolution. Did we waste money? Of course we did, particularly when we threw money at bad governments just because they took our side in the East-West competition. Did we win the battle against poverty? Far from it. All we can claim is that we made the world more livable for millions of people. Imagine what the world would look like today if we hadn't made that effort. Yet, sadly, the world doesn't allow us to sit back and enjoy the benefits of our hard labor. Instead, the world today requires us to do even more. The facts are distressing, but they show clearly that civilization is running on a metaphorical treadmill. If we stop running, we will be thrown into chaos.

"We Americans are more prosperous than ever before but we no longer feel safe. In a world where 10 percent of the people control 90 percent of the wealth, we cannot feel safe. We are threatened by more than just Al-Qaida. We are threatened by the ability of terrorists to exploit pervasive poverty, by their ability to hide and operate in poor countries. We are threatened by failed states, by ethnic conflict and by ordinary people leaving their homes en masse to find food and jobs in the world's burgeoning cities. . . .We can barely manage events today. What will we do in 10 years when the earth's 6 billion people become 7 billion?

Is there something America has forgotten or discarded since Harry Truman, something that can very seriously affect our future?

Atwood thinks there is. In opening the chutes for that outpour of American aid after World War II, he said:

"Truman was telling the country: We Americans, to be true to our own values, must share our know-how and our resources with the underdeveloped world, with that one-half of the world's population that suffered from poverty and misery . . . In retrospect, Harry Truman was doing something quite natural for most Americans. He was reflecting values he learned growing up in the Midwest. He also knew, however, that pervasive world poverty was a time bomb that could disrupt commerce, be exploited by anti-democratic ideologies and produce new wars in which U.S. soldiers would have to fight. Harry Truman's Point 4 program was thus a perfect blend of American values and American interests."

Foreign aid today doesn't have throngs of zealous fans in either the American Congress or on Main Street. Many Americans still imagine the American international aid to be near that 15 to 20 percent of the federal budget of 50 years ago and wonder why we keep pouring money into the pockets of people who don't like us. They are surprised to learn, Brian Atwood noted, that "among the western donor countries, we are by far the least generous as a percentage of our GDP (gross domestic product) per capita. The average American family contributes $40 a year to our foreign aid budget, as opposed to about $800 a year for the average Danish family."

Those numbers, of course, reflect the family's share of the American government's aid to poor countries. What individuals can do or want to do privately is another matter. And what they do privately, and what groups of individuals and corporations do privately, may become very important to the health of the world down the road.

The Bush administration does have a plan, its $5 billion Millennium Challenge Account in potential aid to countries in need. Atwood likes it, but worries about it. The grants from this program would be awarded to countries making the kind of political reforms pleasing to the American quasi-governmental agency that decides who gets the money, which basically means meeting the standards of the administration in power. For Atwood, those standards may "come across as paternalistic (and) increase resentment and achieve little new reform."

All of this is makes microcredit look more inviting than it already is as the most reliable vehicle around to bring food to starving people, to put millions more kids in school, to take millions more out of poverty, and to build political stability in the world.

It satisfies one more fundamental need among those Americans who feel frozen out of their country's political process after watching megamillions of dollars dominate the elections and dominate the country's lawmaking. These are people who constantly ask: "What can one person do? What can I do?" For the American who is bothered by the United States' international behavior, there is an answer. Although the American congress likes the self-help, capitalist concept of microcredit and will offer support, government alone in this country isn't going to give enough to expand microcredit to where it can achieve its professed goal of reaching 100 million of the poorest families by 2005. That is the year that has been designated by the United Nations as its Year of Microcredit. Private organizations, foundations, and individuals will have to make the difference.

The most powerful resource toward this goal, ironically, dwells in the poor themselves. That resource is their yearning to make something of their lives. It is the same yearning as ours, the strengths and drives within us. With some of them it might have been suppressed by their poverty-induced apathy. But with most, that drive can be reawakened. Someone, something can revive that strength. That resilience in the human spirit is no different from yours or mine. What makes us different is opportunity, which often comes down simply to where we were born.

CHAPTER 4

A Professor on a White Horse

The godfather of microcredit around the world is an unquenchable economics professor named Muhammad Yunus of Bangladesh, whose credits may be unique in modern history. Millions of people owe their better lives to his work and his audacity. Scores of millions in the years ahead may say the same.

The movement he evangelized is nothing less than a revolution of the spirit (pumping vitality into the minds and hearts of the poor) combined with Yunus' aggressive insistence that the fundamental rules of the free market mean what they say. They apply equally to berry pickers in Central Asia and venture capitalists in London. To get started, you have to borrow money. If you work hard enough and your mind is creative enough, you'll make headway. If you repay the loans, you'll get another loan. But it all starts with access to capital.

When Yunus talks about bringing a civil life and simple human justice to people who've never had it, his mind races over barriers and through walls and around stagnating traditions. For the last 30 years he has been microcredit's town crier, its Merlin, and its professor on a white horse. Those varied robes have made him a roaming citizen of the world, welcome in the highest councils of practically every government on earth. Why? His cause and message has no real enemies. It has achieved on all continents and it brings something good to almost everything it touches.

He is a bouncy, tireless man with a shrewd and nimble mind and eclectic style that endears him both to financial heavyweights and to paupers. After his studies brought him to America, he returned to Bangladesh in the mid-1970s to found what became the cornerstone of the microcredit system, the Grameen Bank. He did it in the face of some consternation and disbelief from the conventional banking lodge.

You can't let these barefoot women just walk into a bank, they said. You can't give credit to penniless people and do it without their personal collateral.

But he did. It's now being done over most of the world. The collateral isn't the conventional family jewelry. The multitudes of women who get these small loans don't own property. The collateral is the loyalty (and cash) of their circle of banking neighbors.

"We are demonstrating that poor people can take money, take credit, pay back at high repayment rates," he said in a TV program of Word-Pictures and the Worldview International Foundation. "(Credit) can change their life. They don't have to depend on anybody. They're not asking for mercy from anybody. They simply need a fair chance and a fair deal and justice."

He couldn't talk existing banks in Bangladesh into taking a chance on the poor. He became their personal guarantor. Sometimes he drew money out of a bank and gave it to poor people who wanted to buy seed to sell or fish to cook or yarn to spin. He collected the paybacks himself and returned the money to the bank. Eventually he *created* a bank in Bangladesh for millions of people.

There's a reason 90 percent of the clients in microcredit throughout the world are women. Most of them are mothers. Their kids are deprived. The incentive for them to make it, to sell their seed or buy more cows or make more dresses, becomes the dominate force in their lives. The health and future of their kids are the stake in whether they repay that loan or not. So they repay, more often than men do.

Muhammad Yunus again:

"My allegation against the existing banking system (in developing countries) was that it was basically an anti-woman institution. It doesn't lend money to women. If you take all of the borrowers of a bank together (in conventional banks in poor countries) you find only 1 per cent who are women. So when I began I wanted to make sure that I don't make the same mistake. So we (were) trying to achieve an equal number of both men and women. We noticed very remarkable things happening in the families where we lend money to the women. In those families, more benefits are coming than in the families where we gave money to the men."

And Yunus recites this working creed:

"We can remove poverty from the surface of the earth only if we can redesign our institutions—like the banking institutions and others, if we redesign our policies, if we look back on our concepts so that we have a different idea of poor people . . . Credit is a human right that should be treated as a human right. If credit can be accepted as a human right, then all other human rights will be easier to establish . . . Poor people are looked upon as if they have to be dependent on somebody's handout. They are not looking for somebody's handout or somebody's mercy. They want their legitimate due, and they can handle the rest themselves. They can pull themselves out of poverty."

The name of Muhammad Yunus surfaces inevitably whenever the microcredit lodge meets—in chic conference centers in Manhattan where the managers and prophets of microcredit gather, or in the spare one-desk-with-computer offices of the native entrepreneurs in Africa, South America, and Asia. Yunus literally wrote the book of today's microcredit. He was one of 14 children—five of whom died in infancy—of a family living in Chittagong in what was then Eastern Bengal and is now Bangladesh. Chittagong was alive with business action, and Yunus studied at the university there, later won a Fulbright scholarship for advanced studies at Vanderbilt, and then became head of the economics department at Chittagong. He needed no research to understand the massive poverty in that part of the world and the desperate need for some new system to give people of ambition a fighting chance to pull themselves out of the nowhere of their lives. He was aware of the traditional concepts of group or village banking, but he also knew there were only scattered outcroppings of that and that somebody or some institution needed to pioneer in broadening the access of poor people to small amounts of money on credit.

One day in a small village of Bangladesh in the mid 1970s, Yunus delved into his pockets and loaned money to 42 women in that village, most of them stool makers who needed cash they didn't have in order to buy more bamboo to sell more stools. The money Yunus loaned amounted to less than $30. That's the *total* for 42 women.

They bought the material. They made more stools. And they repaid the loans.

That was the beginning of the celebrated Grameen Bank of Bangladesh, Yunus' creation, which within ten years had become the primary model for microcredit managers around the world.

Commercial bankers who are tempted to sniff at Yunus' unorthodoxy in launching a banking business for the poor should open a book of American banking history and turn to a section headed "A.P. Giannini."

Amadeo Peter Giannini was the son of Italian immigrants who settled in California in the late 1800s. Historians and bankers both will quickly identify A.P. Giannini as one of the genuine superstars of the America banking industry, the founder of the Bank of America. Now put an overlay on the personalities and philosophies of Giannini and Muhammad Yunus, whose careers evolved more than a half century apart, and set them side by side.

The similarities in the lines are uncanny. Like Yunus, Giannini was a restless, driven innovator with a supreme belief that banking did not have to be reserved for the comfortably fixed and the corporately entrenched. That mindset characterized banking's field of operation and credit bias in America a hundred years ago. Giannini's Bank of Italy was one of the reputable banks in San Francisco in the early 1900s. When the earthquake struck, most of the city's banks were temporarily shuttered. But Giannini quickly gathered his bank's gold and cash, put it in a horse-drawn wagon and set up a bank in the Italian section of town, making instant small loans to the jobless and now homeless immigrants and asking as collateral "only a signature or your face."

Eventually his Bank of America pioneered in inviting depositors and lenders who came from the ranks of the less prosperous. All right, let's use the word "poor," a word that ought not to be confined to the non-western world. This core belief in democratizing banking, both in the social rightness and the profitability of that idea, made the Bank of America truly national in reach.

Giannini's act of trust in offering banking credit to the Italian immigrants defined a simple but profound truth of the human spirit when it is united with opportunity. The building of America is marbled with the faces and legends of men and women who raised themselves, with one small loan, from modest origins or actual penury to a successs that transformed the lives of multitudes. It's one reason why it should be so natural for American capitalists and Americans in general to applaud the ethic of microcredit for the world's poor.

In the pits of the Great Depression, the son of a Minneapolis grocer borrowed $55 to market a sales-enhancing promotion for grocery stores. Give your customers trading stamps as a reward for their business and their loyalty, he told them. The stamps could be redeemed for a varity of gift merchandise. Curt Carlson was in his 20s and freshly graduated from the University of Minnesota. He didn't invent the idea of trading stamps but he focused his promotion on grocery stores and he did it energetically and creatively. He called his product Gold Bond Stamps. Within a couple of years Gold Bond Stamps were lining the premium booklets of American customers from coast to coast. The idea lives today in a dozen different incarnations in American industry and has long since gone airborne in the form of frequent flyer miles for airline travel. Carlson eventually sold his highly productive trading stamp business and became a hotelier with his flagship Radisson hotels. In 1973 he created Carlson Companies, an extraordinary international conglomerate that by the turn of the century had developed annual revenues of more than $20 billion and employed a workforce of 160,000. Its corporate reach includes the ownership and management of hotels, travel agencies, restaurant chains, incentive vacations, cruise ships and more.

Curt Carlson died in 1999. He never forgot his Swedish forebears or his business ethic and creed: "Reach as high as you can; if you miss getting to the stars, at least you reach the moon." His reach ultimately including the giving of tens of millions of dollars to the University of Minnesota and other institutions and the creation of a foundation that reflected his global visions and concepts of giving.

Carlson understood that humans who are poor and ambitions can yearn for something beyond them, to fly to the moon, as intensely as those with a launching pad as big and fulfilling as the United States. The woman at her loom in India is never going to run a conglomerate. Nobody is going stage a banquet for her and invite thousands to join in tribute when her work is done. Her hunger to succeed is as powerful as the drive that propelled AP Giannini and Curt Carlson. Until microcredit, there was practically no hope for her to make something of her life and the lives of her children. There is now. Her banquet is the smile on the face of her youngest, who can now eat adequately. It is the books in the hands of her older children, who can now read and write. It is the gratitude she feels for having a chance to change her life, and doing it. And she got the chance because somebody trusted her to repay a $40 loan.

Which she did.

What microcredit was in the beginning, the group lending idea, is essentially what it is today. The numbers in the groups are often bigger, but the principle is the same. The group is the collateral for all of the individual members who borrow at interest. When Yunus drew the plan, a person who wanted to take out a loan had to find four other people for partners, none of them family members.

At the start, the idea was for two of the group members to get credit up to $100 or so and often less. If they were successful and repaid the loans, the others qualified. All transactions were done strictly within the view of all members of the group, creating an atmosphere of trust and transparency from the beginning. The interest rate of 20 percent in the early days of Grameen also became a model for the microcredit groups that followed, but those rates now vary with economic conditions and practice in different parts of the world where microcredit operates.

Eventually Grameen, as a giant Bank of the People, came to serve more than 2 million borrowers. In Bangladesh, specifically, it was followed by aggressive competitors who have swelled the number of microcredit borrowers in that country alone to the range of 10 million. Yunus became a charismatic, patriarchal figure in microcredit, a man about whom books were written and whose commentary and judgments acquired a kind of gospel power.

So there was some dismay in the microcredit community when the Wall Street Journal published a story in November of 2001 raising questions about the recent performance of Grameen. Grameen, it noted, had been declaring on its web site that loan repayments averaged over 95 percent—the same figure widely used among microcredit advocates the world over to characterize their own performance. That figure remains an accurate measure of microcredit's repayment record, including Grameen's in normal conditions.

But, the Journal said, Grameen's performance in recent years "hasn't lived up to the bank's own hype." It cited Grameen's own figures to show that 19 percent of recent loans were overdue, "giving it a delinquency rate more than twice the often-cited level of less than 5 percent."

Considering the stresses in Bangladesh at the time, that repayment rate, although temporarily below the microcredit standard established by Grameen itself, was hardly a punk performance. The Journal acknowledged that microcredit was an idea that everyone could agree on. It liked the idea that microcredit is based on solid practices of private enterprise, that it can be profitable, and that it gets money straight to the poor. Grameen's problems, it said, may have flowed from its success: it was and is so good and grew so hugely that imitators and competitors moved in. Grameen had additional manage-rial troubles resulting from its size.

Yunus acknowledged that Grameen had been having some repayment glitches during a period of political upheavals and floods in Bangladesh. He said Grameen had been tardy in deleting from the web the reference to a repayment rate of "over 95" percent and it had tightened up reporting procedures. He'd willingly made all figures available to the newspaper. Still, he said, 85 percent of the borrowers had repaid every week and the others would repay their delinquent notes. He called the bank "stronger than ever."

The response from friends of Grameen and from microcredit advocates in general was to deplore what they regarded as a cheap shot dismissing of Grameen's decades-long achievement in lifting hundreds of thousands of people out of poverty. It had done so, they said, under the daunting conditions of life in one of the world's poorer countries. Yunus himself offered this non-inflammatory defense of his monu-mental work, the Grameen: "Where others see overdue loans, we see hard-working, struggling women who have demonstrated their capa-bility to repay loans many times over, and who have saved $114 mil-lion—and we know we have good reasons to feel confident. We remember that 85 percent of our borrowers are paying with clock-work precision. Only 15 percent are having difficulties—and we know that external factors (the flood, political turmoil) caused those difficulties. (They will repay their loans) and we will solve the prob-lems, just as we have many times before."

That this huge structure of credit to the poor was able to with-stand extraordinary duress and still operate successfully and respon-sively speaks powerfully for its staying power. Less could be said for the performance of many high-end financial institutions under compa-rable stress—as we've seen in the early twenty-first century.

The liberation of poor women that Yunus' and his pioneering has fostered and the new life his model has given to millions remains one of the dramatic sagas of the war on poverty of the twentieth century. And it presents the authentic promise of even greater breakthroughs in the twenty-first.

Among some economists there is still a lot of sophisticated resistance to this peppery mix of banking idealism and combative populism. But those words roll off the skin of people Anna Setoko, an African woman whose story tells you more about microcredit at its best than the economists can. She was 24 when her husband died in

Tanzania, leaving her with eight children and a small plot of maize. She didn't have enough money to clothe her children or to buy seeds for her little plantation. In the midst of that duress she heard about an organization called Pride Tanzania, a microfinance agency that receives funds from donors and makes small loans available to people like Anna.

After she took out her first loan, she said, she started buying maize. "When I started I could never afford more than 10 bags," she said. "Now I buy 20 and I have moved into the wholesale business."

She sells now to traders in the main market in Arusha, a major city in north central Tanzania. She also runs a small bar in Merelani, a mining town north of there. She and her family can now afford medical treatment, which was impossible before. Her children dress well. Her oldest daughter, now 20, was recently married. Life for Anna Setoko and all those who depended on her has never been better.

And there was a time not so long ago when nobody would let her inside a bank.

You can multiply Anna Setoko's story into the millions, because microcredit's most profound gift has been to the repressed women of the world. That gift, it should be noted, has been largely shaped in the Islamic land of Bangladesh under a leadership—Muhammad Yunus'— that declined to flinch in the face of cultural tradition and economic taboos.

CHAPTER 5

A Village Rescues the Orphans of AIDS

K ampala, Uganda—

An American walking across the tiny red clay parking lot on a visit to the Nsambya hospital in Kampala has to fight off his stereotypes.

Our images of Africa are overwhelmed by scenes of sickness, starvation, war, and corruption. The pictures are hard to erase even among those who have traveled there and know that sub-Saharan Africa, for all of its suffering and turmoil, is not a place of unrelieved torment.

But here in the hospital was the face of a man to shake that fixed imagery. He was dying of AIDS. Yet in an unforeseeable turnabout in his life, a new world had opened up for him in his native Uganda, had in fact lengthened and deepened his life without the benefit of the life-saving drugs that rescued thousands in prosperous western nations. Perhaps symbolically, it has happened for Godfrey Mukasa and others not far from the source of the great life-giver of Africa, the River Nile.

He had been a soldier in the gruesome civil wars of the Uganda bush in the 1980s, Godfrey Mukasa, wounded in the struggle that ultimately brought his people a semblance of peace and independence at the turn of the new millennium.

Later he was raising a family when a trauma even more brutal than the rampages of Idi Amin struck Uganda.

His body and life have been scarred by both. First it was the cyclical warfare and intramural slaughter of the Amin and Milton Obote regimes. And he is now marked by the epic scourge of HIV-AIDS that has threatened to turn sub-Saharan Africa into a vast morgue from the Red Sea to the Atlantic to the continent's southernmost outreach, ironically called The Cape of Good Hope.

And yet his was not the face of hopelessness; nor does Uganda strike the visitor as a wasteland of fatalism and despair. With a choice of giving up or maximizing every day left to him, Godfrey Mukasa—with the aid of a small loan—began a business. He began to care for his body and to counsel those around him. To understand what has happened to Mukasa and to others like him, and to understand what is possible, you have to shake loose from some of those pre-conceptions of today's Africa and some of our illusions about what should be done.

This is a place—most of Africa, Uganda in particular—that has already experienced its Armageddon: the slaughters of the civil wars, then starvation, and then AIDS and the aftershocks of all of them. The illusions begin with a presumption by potential benefactors (and these people *do* need benefactors). The presumption is that we can assert a higher moral ground than the dysfunctional countries we deal with. The illusion is that we can impose on them a political order and eager democracy as a condition for putting Africa on its feet economically and stamping out poverty. Helping these people and their struggling new nations is a mission that makes sense humanely and gives us the added, hard-headed incentive of advancing our own interests. But if you share that belief, then you have to begin by adjusting your sights. We can't help them to salvage their struggling independence on one hand and as part of the bargain force them to clone our institutions to make theirs look and act like ours right now, today. That Utopia may come. It's not going to come to Africa tomorrow, or the day after or the year after. But a more decent and fulfilling life for millions of its people can.

Some of the best of Africa's new beginnings, rough-hewn and improvised and yet somehow brave and full of resolution, are here in Uganda, a land battered almost beyond all identity as a recognizable nation-state just 20 years ago.

Godfrey Mukasa might be its symbol.

You don't have to be naïve about looking at Africa today or ignore the scale of grief facing it. No part of the world has suffered from the plague of HIV-AIDS as horrendously. In the year 2002, the count of people infected with HIV stood at 22 million. The number of orphans of AIDS in Africa reached beyond 12 million in 2002. The World Health Organization reported in May that 6,000 young people between the ages of 15 and 24 and 2,000 youngsters under 15 were infected daily. Half of the countries are bankrupt. Some are still controlled by generals and homicidal dictators. The poverty, the massive tragedy of AIDS and the gropings of even its more responsible leaders to find a way to stability still mock the heroic slogans of the leaders who wrested Africa's independence from the colonial overlords in the 1950s and 1960s. Somebody called Africa the real Lost Continent.

Is it that? My wife, Susan Wilkes, and I went back to East Africa in the spring of 2002, to find out if the despair and turmoil are so deep that no amount of money or good will can extricate it.

We didn't see that.

But we saw something else in Africa in the spring of 2002, and it needs to be reported. We saw Africans building new lives, led by trained and charismatic African managers of credit and grants, supported by American and European donors, non-profit organizations, and entrepreneurs. I'm no authority on the African scene. I've led photo safaris and climbs on Kilimanjaro over the years, walked 200 miles in the African Rift with a handful of fundraisers to build a money pool for schools, and pursued elephant poachers with the Tanzanian park rangers. I'm drawn to Africa's wild nature and the struggles and potential of its people. Susan is the manager of family foundations, a longtime advocate in international development and a friend of Africa. We went back in the spring of 2002 to explore the value of microcredit in a land torn the last 50 years by convulsions on a Biblical scale. Some of the scenes we do not want to forget and will not, and one of the Africans was Godfrey Mukasa.

He sat quietly in the small hospital in Kampala, waiting to receive what medicines the caretakers could provide. Outside the clinic entry, on wooden benches only partly shielded from the equatorial sun, nearly 25 men, women and youngsters waited to be called for whatever treatment or comfort was available. All of them had tested positive for HIV-AIDS. Some of the women wore their best and most colorful *kangas,* the traditional garment of East Africa. The floral designs that splashed in oranges and greens across the cloth softened the somber sculpture of their faces, some of which were truly and dramatically beautiful.

Some of the faces Susan and I saw were not those of the stereotypes. They belonged to Africans who—for all of the heartbreak of HIV and AIDS—are living more humanely today than they did a year ago because they have access to money that they didn't have then. The money comes as a loan through microcredit and is being used by a growing number of AIDS victims or their families to build or enlarge small enterprises in the street market or at home. They use it for clothes and food and school for their children, and to care for the orphans of AIDS in their extended families.

Their story belongs not only in their villages, but in our lives as well, because what Africa has been enduring is a global catastrophe. A generation has lost half of its teachers. Youngsters have been orphaned by the millions. Most African governments make a ceremonial bow to democracy but put more trust and comfort in one-party rule— meanings theirs. Yet there are ways that Africa's malaise can be and is being confronted, and they make sense to the western mind that prizes initiative and reward for effort. American banking executives, fascinated by the extraordinary repayment performance by the little people who take out loans, like to call microcredit a tribute to the capitalist ideal. It is partly that. But there is also a sizeable amount of heart in it and, if the corporate captains don't mind, perhaps more guts and brains than they realize.

Most of the people in this small hospital in Uganda, though, know about it. Godfrey Mukasa, the soldier, and the patients on those benches do. Susan and I walked across the lot, trying to be unobtrusive, restraining our sympathy because that isn't what they seemed to want or need. What they needed was something not available to them, the near-miracle drugs that have prolonged the lives of HIV-AIDS victims in the northern hemispheres. We saw almost no animation in the eyes of the patients, and barely a hint of curiosity as we walked to the hospital entrance. Well, why should there be? These people were poor, sick, and struggling to hang on. We said "jambo, habari." Hello. How are you?

What they needed was hope, if not for a substantial extension of their lives, then at least a relief from the quiet terror that had hung over them and their children until they arrived at the Nysamba hospital to enter a program started by a Scottish priest in 1991.

And there, something changed in their lives. For them the hospital has become a place of welcome and nurture, and an embrace. It does not produce miracles. Some of the men and women we passed on the benches will die soon. Yet none seemed in total despair. They looked ahead, some with a stoical patience, others in anticipation of meeting a friend.

A friend, in a hospital where most of them were going to postpone a premature death?

Yes, that. To them she is Beatrice, a lifeline. Beatrice Lubega manages the hospital's social service, called AIDS Widows Orphans

Family Support (AWOFS). It gives the victims of AIDS a will to live, a chance to use small grants and loans to bring in income that can put the orphans of AIDS in a schoolroom or to build their skills for jobs that will keep their younger siblings together. It is a simple but breathtaking concept.

And now around the country of Uganda add thousands of volunteers to serve as foster parents. Suddenly for a country that had been reeling under the successive hammer blows of civil war and AIDS, a new vitality and cause have emerged: making a life for its millions of orphans. The country's first lady, Janet Museveni, pioneered the Uganda Women's Effort to Save Orphans, UWESO. Is this one more clumsy acronym to add to the alphabet jungle? Well, no. These are grandmothers, working women, tired women who live an axiom that one remembers best from a visit to Africa. It cuts across all of Africa's intramural strife and struggle and rhetorically at least unites its people.

"Every child should have a mother, and will."

That, too, is breathtaking.

Slogans can be beautiful. This one is. But in a country like Uganda, pounded and traumatized by war and AIDS, the slogan is an empty hope without massive resolve and sacrifice.

It is also empty without women like Beatrice Lubega of the AWOFS organization operating the AIDS hospital in Kampala.

Beatrice radiates nonstop energy and vast working knowledge of the human condition. She is a confessor for some, a backbone for others as well as friend and confidante. She had something for each of her AIDS patients on this day. To a woman in her 20s, Beatrice talked positively about the week ahead; and to a frail, middle-aged man, she offered a plan to bring extra money into his household for the care of his children. The hospital's work and the loan and grant programs for its patients are supported or funded by several church agencies, the Belgian Fund, Trickle-Up, the McKnight Foundation, and UNICEF, among others. In the hospital's reception room we found Godfrey, an Army veteran of 37, once married, once the father of three. A few years ago his wife died. Meningitis was officially listed as the cause of death. He knows it was AIDS.

Not long ago his youngest child, a girl of seven died of malaria. His wound, suffered in a firefight in the Ugandan jungle years ago when he was an infantry lieutenant in the National Resistance Army, will not heal because he, too, has been diagnosed with HIV-AIDS.

Godfrey was willing to talk frankly about his life. Most of the AIDS patients are. His English was strong but quiet and reflective. His eyes were serious and probing and didn't suggest a man resigned to a fatal illness. He said:

"When my wife died, I went in to be tested and found out I was infected. Here that almost always means death. There didn't seem to be anything left for me. We had a good marriage. She was a fine person and mother. The world fell apart. I had a long period of sadness when I didn't do anything. But I talked to the hospital people and a counselor here, and they said that I already knew the worst and there were two ways to face it. Give up or try to live. I had gone through all of the phases of shock and denying and being bitter. Now I had to accept. I could say I was going to die soon. But I still had two children.

"The workers here said look at the reality of life. The first thing you know is that it's going to be shorter. But if you dig into yourself and find out what's still possible, it can be better when you're serving something or somebody. I started with that. I took a small loan from one of the credit groups and built up a café in my house on the edge of the city. It's doing OK, enough to put my two children in boarding school. I see them two or three times a week. I talked to them as honestly as I could. I said I had a plan for their schooling and I thought I could live for ten years longer, maybe more. I started to take care of myself with exercise and living sensibly. I put in long hours at the restaurant. I stopped smoking and drinking alcohol. I entered this credit group and I decided to be an example. I'm the chairman of a hospital patients' support group. I try to stay optimistic. If I have any thing wrong with my body, I report it right away. I can't afford the good drugs. They would cost $200 a month. I don't have sex. That would be an awful thing to do. But each day I tell myself I'm getting things done. My life now is my children's future. I feel like I'm a whole person again."

So here was a place where you have to discard your preconceptions about Africa. There was something in that hospital, there is something about thousands of healthy women building their own small businesses in Kampala, in Arusha, Tanzania, in the countryside of Kenya, that challenges the horror pictures we carry in the sanctuary of our comfortable lives.

But in Africa the overpowering life-or-death struggle is AIDS. There isn't enough money and there are almost no drugs worth the name to deal with it. Africa needs massive infusion of western medicines and care and money. But it's not hopeless when AIDS encounters people like Rumalati Kibirge, a woman of Wanyanga in Uganda. Her 22-year-old daughter died of AIDS, leaving her to care for the young woman's four children. Later Rumalati's sisters died. And quite suddenly Rumalati Kibirge's home filled with 15 children, most of them orphaned by AIDS.

She was already operating a tiny business, baking and selling pastries the Ugandans call *sumbusa, chapati,* and *mandazi.* But now with 15 youngsters to feed and clothe and educate, she went to a village banking group called Akanabala affiliated with the FINCA microfinance agency. She asked for a loan and received it—for $35. In America, $35 can buy you a movie for two and a couple of medium bags of popcorn. In Rumalati's ledgers it meant buying baking ingredients in bulk to take advantage of wholesale prices, which meant a few cents more profit. Those few cents go a lot further in Africa than in an American shopping mall. They become the equivalent of extra dollars and dozens of more customers and then three larger loans until she'd borrowed $317.

Of that, she saved $270 for food and clothes for the children, medicine, and fees at school. That didn't leave her with much cash to re-invest in her business. But she knew, and her village bank knew, that she was good for loans. And it helped that FINCA, one of the most respected microcredit providers, offered her a menu of outpatient services and life insurance.

It offered her one more value: the confidence she acquired taking on those huge new responsibilities and responding to them as she did. "I used to not be able to speak in front of people," she said. "I was afraid. I'm not afraid any more."

That is the microcredit model. It is not unflawed. Sometimes it's hard for the providers to reach the poorest. Sometimes the system becomes overly dependent on donors. Yet it has been extraordinarily flexible, and it is battle-proven. It is global and adapts to most cultural and ethnic models. At Beatrice Lubega's hospital for AIDS victims in Kampala, it's true, economic models don't mean much. Saving life and giving a civilized meaning to the remaining years of the dying mean more. But the spirit implicit in the ideal of microcredit—treating poor and struggling people with the same trust and respect you give to the well off—has moved this innovative little hospital to use small grants and loans as a cornerstone of a commitment. That commitment, in the midst of the AIDS crisis, is to one of the most fundamental of all medical ethics: to care for the suffering, the dying, but not to overlook the needs of the living, their survivors. And that has become a national gospel in a place like Uganda.

Beatrice Lubega:

"I have to tell you first how it is each day. You can't afford to be depressed. We're not. There is too much to do. There are too many lives that can be saved or changed by the small things you can do. First, everybody you know in this part of the world has been touched by AIDS. My family has been. It can break your heart when you see somebody who looks strong come in for treatment. And then they get weaker and weaker. And then there is not much left but skin and bone. That is what AIDS has done. But what we have done in our county, with the help of people outside our country, is to reduce the rate of infection. It's going down. It's going down with sex education. In this hospital when we talk about how to prevent AIDS we talk straight. We talk about condoms and how to use them. We talk about who is the partner. This is a hospital built by people of religion with great vision. We respect that. But we still have to give information about condoms.

"We get involved with the lives of the children and equipping those children for the world by giving them vocational training, skills, with the help of the Trickle Up organization and others." (Trickle Up is a much-admired donor of small grants around the world. Its organizational matriarch is Millie Leet, a revered figure in international aid).

"They will give a grant of $100 for a project if the people who receive it have a plan. So the children of AIDS victims, who are either living with their brothers and sisters or older relatives or foster parents, take training and make a report on it and make themselves eligible for another grant. We also work with organizations that offer small loans to people who have AIDS but who don't want to go home and lay down and die. They want to do something with their hands or minds that will keep them busy and help their children. They buy things to sell in the market or to make something out of wood or cloth. All of that gives them hope and a reason for living. We have programs teaching them how to make their wills so that their children are provided for with the property the parents can pass on. If they don't do it legally, sometimes relatives can just grab the property."

Because of the hard realities like that, people who presume to provide aid and direction in Africa can't afford sugar-and-spice language when they talk about the scale of the AIDS struggle or the answers. The microfinance agency Opportunity International puts it bluntly and offers one response that goes to the heart of a male-dominant cultural pattern that has contributed powerfully to the crisis:

"The AIDS epidemic is decimating the face of Africa. It is killing whole generations of mothers and fathers and leaving a sea of orphans in its wake . . . If the AIDS awareness has not reduced the rate of infection (although it some parts of Africa it has) the question that still must be answered is this: what other factors, apart from HIV-ignorance, are contributing to the high rates of HIV in certain African countries? Because many women are economically dependent on men, the degree to which they are able to express their own will is often limited. This lack of choice—or lack of power—leads some women to engage in high-risk behaviors, which increase their chance of contracting the HIV virus. Many women believe the negative economic consequences of leaving the high-risk relationship outweigh the possible repercussions of staying with an infected partner."

Which means, Opportunity International is convinced, that women are afraid of ending up destitute and alone if they walk out on a partner who is HIV-infected. So they stay in the marriage or the relationship and become infected themselves.

What it is saying further, is that microcredit can give thousands of these women a way out, and therefore can give them life—and is doing that today. How? By providing small loans that give these endangered women a foothold to independence. It can open a door to a life in which they can support themselves or to support themselves and their children. It also can give them access to life-saving health care, orphan care, and disease prevention programs. These are typically offered through partnerships of village banking systems and health and education agencies and volunteer networks like the one undertaken on a massive scale by Janet Museveni's UWESO in Uganda.

It was no coincidence that wherever we saw a positive approach or a positive reaction to AIDS in Africa, we saw the picture of microcredit in action. Here was microcredit bringing new income into the homes of foster parents of the AIDS orphans. They are "the mother" every child must have and will have, in the language of that most passionate of all affirmations of the African people. It is new income that can send an AIDS orphan to school, clothe and feed that orphan and make the child part of family. This wasn't a dole to the women foster parents we met. It was a loan, something to build on in creating a new family that they alone—*alone*—can sustain. It does something beyond that. It ends a woman's fears of inadequacy to deal with the consuming grief of AIDS in her village. It creates, in fact, an entirely new world for this woman in the midst of burdens. Facing it as bravely and unselfishly has become her salvation.

Here was microcredit expanding the life of Godfrey Mukasa in the very years when he was dying, giving him the motivation, the work and the society of others in a way that both revitalized him and made him an inspiration to others.

And here was microcredit, primarily in the form of a village banking group, giving the potential victims of disease the kind of information that could keep them healthy by making them aware of their vulnerability and how to care for themselves

Essentially, in this most terrible of all crises, the microcredit system has worked to reduce the horror and to redirect hundreds of thousands of lives. It has faults and issues, but it will extend the life of a Godfrey Mukasa. And it will make life more civilized and humane for tens of thousands of others, beginning with a generation of orphans.

CHAPTER 6

She Flew Down the Mountain in Her Bowler Hat

L a Paz, Bolivia—

A mountaineer can look up at the snow mountains of the Andes and tingle with the prospect of climbing their dazzling ice walls. That is part of the hypnotic power of South America: white mountains thrusting into the blue sub-stratosphere, grand but lonely.

An anthropologist can look into the faces of the mixed bloods of the Andean people and be instantly immersed in the antiquity of their civilizations. That is part of allure of South America.

But an ordinary visitor to South America can look into the same faces and be quietly enraged by the cycles of cruelty and exploitation that have beaten down these people for centuries. That is part of the historic tragedy of South America.

It doesn't matter whether it was imposed by conquistadors, power-drunk generals and military juntas, misdirected religious fervor, fortune-hunting foreign capitalists, or drug barons. The masses of people in South America have never emerged from historic poverty.

But it does not have to be an unrelieved prison for them, a life sentence to hard labor and hunger.

Nobody knows this better than a woman named Carmen Velasco, who has strode the Andean foothills for years with her ledgers and passbooks and her hard-headed invitation to women: "You can accept being doormats for the rest of your lives. Or you can come with us." One can picture Carmen Velasco as a kind of trench-fighting Joan of Arc in the garments of Mother Hubbard, showing the way for thousands of women to dig themselves out of obscurity. That picture is accurate, but it might be inadequate. You don't bring more money into tens of thousands of households without knowing something basic about banking, economics, and psychology, and about the time for discipline and leadership and the time for a strategic hug.

The workings of microcredit, how it's analyzed and evaluated, usually are the dominion of high-level economists and the wizards of money handling in dozens of workshop conferences every year. But to understand the emotional and financial impact it has on the slow and often grudging emancipation of women around the world, you'd need to meet Carmen Velasco.

The struggle of women to gain the same rights, power, and basic dignity probably began with Eve. Carmen Velasco will scowl if you bring up that familiar allusion to Eve as the first female victim. What woman wants the dubious original sin of humanity fastened on a woman—again? What Carmen Velasco knows is how to take a relatively small microcredit organization called Pro Mujer and to give it vitality and reach and everyday relevance in the life of poor women of the Andes, and to somehow make them women of the world in what they have achieved in their lives. Another thing she knows and preaches is that the money they get to build a little business, in the outdoor market or inside the bare walls of their homes, is not a dole.

They have to pay it back at interest to get another loan. If they don't, they wash out as borrowers. Remember, also, that these are tiny enterprises. They mean hawking stuff, sewing it, cooking it, milking cows, feeding pigs, and a hundred other things. Because most of the loans go to women, it doesn't mean men don't qualify. But women get most of the loans for some pretty practical reasons.

Here is Robin Ratcliffe, the communications vice president for ACCION, one of the powerhouses in microcredit in South America and elsewhere, explaining why it's women who built the successes of microcredit:

> "The women (we studied) were found to invest less of their profits in the business itself. Instead, they invest their profits in their children and in their families. Women don't drink or gamble or otherwise fritter away their profits. They put it back in their business, and they definitely put it back in the well-being of their children, both in nutrition and schooling and in housing."

She has this advice for people who operate microfinance institutions:

"Hire more women as senior managers . . . Many organizations are not only run by men, but they have not offered women
important positions in the management structure. There is
really no better way to make a microenterprise development
gender-oriented than to have women in strong management
positions. Women are by nature more likely to set the agenda
of looking at gender issues, and women will more easily mentor other women within the organization."

One of those mentoring women is the highly energetic and
inventive Carmen Velasco, who lives in La Paz and directs the Bolivian
segment of Pro Mujer (translated "for women"), which serves some
40,000 clients, 97 percent of them women. All of them live in the
mountain country of northern Bolivia, primarily in the urban area
around La Paz. La Paz is typical of the metropolitan centers in the
developing countries. The rural villages are practically dried up as the
providers of services and whatever opportunity there is in those low
end jobs of the poorest countries. So the villagers flee to the big cities,
which are already filled with their own poor and now are flooded with
the migrant poor.

There they find practically no new jobs. La Paz, with a population of 900,000 a few years ago, has been bloated with another
700,000 or so who have thronged the suburb of El Alto. In the urban
centers in the Andes, the well-off live in the lowest-lying districts, the
ones nearest water. The poor live higher on the mountain. The
incoming poor live in the scrubbiest, barest mountain slopes.

On a summer day in July of 2001, I spent a few hours with
Carmen Velasco and three of her clients. My one regret is that it
wasn't three weeks. If your eyes and ears are open, the ambitious poor
can teach you things about life that you'd never considered when you
loosely used the word "entrepreneur" and summoned photos of Andrew
Carnegie and Henry Ford, the poster boys of entrepreneurship.

No Henry Fords turned up in our explorations in La Paz.
Catalina Quispe and her friends did. Ford made more money. He
couldn't possibly have been as much fun.

From another part of La Paz, where she was escorting foundation
clients, Susan, my wife, wanted to know how my conversation went
with the three Pro Mujer *cholitas*. I emailed her from the Paris Hotel:

"If I'd spent three weeks instead of three hours with them, I could have ridden the greasiest road south of the equator, from La Paz to Chulumani. I could have ridden it with Catalina Quispe and her 200 pounds of dried lamb and pork and cheese. It's what she does as a businesswoman. Call it one more day at the office in the Andes. She doesn't speak English and Carmen translated. Catalina's speed-of-light Spanish instantly loosed waves of Carmen's adrenaline because it was Carmen who launched Catalina on those wild rides years ago. You have to construct a picture of the scene. Catalina is riding in the box of a truck with 79 other passengers. That number is correct. Eighty people in a truck. Try doing a product inventory in a truck rolling down a road in the Andes, dodging mudslides and potholes. Do it while the truck driver reveals no symptoms of slowing down and no special knowledge of the location of the brake."

In a moment we're going to rejoin Catalina and discover what happens when that careening load of meat gets to market, if it survives the chaotic ride. The road drops more than a vertical mile from the frost of La Paz to the subtropics of Chulumani. After six years of hauling her goods through rain, snow and heat, Catalina now seems unshaken by this six-hour trauma, which brings us back to the catalyst in all this, Carmen Velasco. The women she supervises are part of the Pro Mujer solidarity that she helped to create. Alongside some of the brand name international leaders in the microcredit industry, Pro Mujer is a grass roots, folksy operation. But it's in dead earnest and some of it is absolutely a life-of-death matter to families hanging on by a shred. Hunger is lethal in the remote mountains of Bolivia.

Microcredit obviously needs both the big hitters of lending, those speaking for hundreds of thousands of clients, as well as the Pro Mujers. Carmen's clients in Pro Mujer are often neighbors on the block, the poorest of them, a functioning and growing lodge of women who meet weekly to share their strength and trust. They meet to pay their loans and to talk plain language about something very large that has happened in their lives. What has happened is that they have elevated themselves and found a new voice in how they live. They now take risks by accepting those loans and they produce new money they had never foreseen. But you don't have to spend much time with Catalina and her friends to realize that the women in Pro Mujer are something more than small loan customers.

The sociologists call it empowerment. The spin-offs from it are more food and better clothes for the kids, an expanded sense of worth among the women and this new excitement in their lives. The working mothers of El Alto didn't think in terms of ideals when they were grubbing out a living at $1 a day. They didn't have the time or energy to imagine rosier futures for their kids in rags. But they still imagined.

"And now listen to Catalina, Susan. It's something she thinks about today, the years when she was grubbing a few cents a day and sometimes cried when she thought about what would become of her children. Six years ago she began taking her small loans. They were $50 and $100 worth at first and a little more later, money she used to increase the amount of meat she could buy from wholesalers to sell to her customers in Chulumani. Being part of the Pro Mujer network was worth more than the simple credit she got every five or six weeks. "They told me how I could sell better and how I could save money while I was borrowing," she said. "They gave me some ideas about how to keep my three children healthy, and they told me about the rights women should have. It was more than just about money. But now my family is ready to buy a house. The children are all going to school."

"She is a hefty woman, an honest-to-God entrepreneur with a big and generous laugh and the confident bearing of a person who knows she has achieved in the face of oppressive societal tradition—to say nothing of bad roads. Some days the weather on the road to Chulumani gets so lousy, she said, that she has to sleep in the open, with 79 others, while a bulldozer clears the mud.

"But she sells the meat and cheese. Nobody sells it better, Carmen Velasco said. She'd escorted the three women into the lobby of the Hotel Paris in La Paz where we'd arranged to talk. They came wearing the full broad skirts and quirky little bowler hats that identify the women of northern Bolivia, the cholitas. I expected them to come in tentatively. Northern Bolivia is immersed in poverty. The Paris is a venerable and stylish hotel downtown where the waiters move around in tuxedos and white arm towels. But the three cholitas strode in without a blush of timidity and plunked down in the thick lobby chairs.

"These three women had stared down hunger and empty shelves and made their marks. They knew it and felt it. What was a big hotel to them if somebody like Catalina made good bucks riding that slippery road to Chulumani?

"Carmen is a shrewd and amiable woman who knew from the beginning that Pro Mujer couldn't afford grandiose notions of building itself into a big bank. Those 25 or 30 women who gather in the community rooms for their meetings make the decisions on loans. They put up their own money if one of them falls behind. That hasn't changed and isn't likely to. Pro Mujer had to keep its horizons low but broad if it was going to bring something good and permanent into the lives of the poor and predominately working mothers who make up the vast bulk of its growing membership. So it's loans stay around $50 and $100, maybe a little higher if the woman sells like Catalina.

"In a community building in El Alto today are tables laden with 24 new computers, the gift of a family foundation in New York. 'We have graduated 400 young people from the ages of 7 to 14 in our computer classes,' Carmen Velasco said. 'They all are doing better in school than their parents ever imagined.'

"Pro Mujer does mean "for women." But it could hardly emulate macho sexism and freeze out male clients. So it has offered loans to some of the men and found most of them trustworthy and agreeable, but they do remember a weekly committee meeting in El Alto when the cholitas drew a line in the sand. 'The three or four men in the meeting insisted on trying to take over the committee,' Carmen said, 'so the women threw them out.'

"You can call that empowerment. You might even call it the tread of history. It looked more like a crowd of women who had heard that song before and didn't like the lyrics.

"Catalina's friend, Adela Hualuque, began borrowing from Pro Mujer when Carmen and her associates launched it 11 years ago. She made clothing with yarn and wool she bought with her loans. Today one of her daughters is attending the University of La Paz. The other will enroll later this year, and Adela is now a credit supervisor for Pro Mujer. Catalina's other friend, Aracely Portillo, is a 30-year-old woman who sold enough pots and pans and tubs and cleansers to rent her own storefront and who says today:"I feel I'm going higher and higher each day, and life is good for my family, and I didn't think it ever would be."

She got there by borrowing $50 at a time from somebody who trusted her. This is a country wretchedly poor but now finding something, in an idea called Pro Mujer, of enduring value and hope to thousands of families.

This is no fairy tale. These people are real and so is the brutality of life in Bolivia. They can escape its crushing dead ends if they connect their lives to an idea that brings down the barricades raised by history and tradition, and bathes their new road with the light of another world newly revealed to them. For these women, Pro Mujer has kept that path open by insisting that it will not dilute its mission of opening its services and its loan offices to the very poorest. It was a commitment that Carmen Velasco and Lynne Patterson shared when they founded Pro Mujer. Although outweighed by the bigger names in microcredit, it now numbers thousands of clients in Mexico, Nicaragua, Bolivia, and Peru. It does that with the energy and inventiveness provided by Velasco in South America and Patterson, the coordinator in New York. And although it lacks huge operating capital, Pro Mujer will often enter a partnership with other providers and work the extra hour to give its clients the health guidance, family planning, and education that the loan by itself cannot provide.

What stirs most poor women in the midst of this true transformation is a memory. They remember earlier in their own lives, or certainly the lives of their mothers and grandmothers, when the woman of the house or shack was the one who got up at 4:00 in the morning to walk a half mile to the river for water. She carried the water in a bucket on her head or in pails hanging from a yoke around her neck. She was the one who boiled the water, cooked the food, fed the pigs or milked the cows if there were cows to milk, dressed the children if there were clothes for them to wear. She washed and hung the clothes; she made the rest of the meals, mothered the children and was the last to go to sleep.

It was the social norm of the low-end family. This isn't to say the man of the place was a beast. More often then not he was and is the provider, or one of the providers. In fact, it wasn't much different in early America or, come to think of it, nineteenth century America. But millions of women in the poorest, most primitive societies, often in the tribal societies, experienced scant relief and never saw wider horizons until the microcredit revolution arrived.

A smaller lending enterprise like Pro Mujer needs enough assets to meet the disproportionate cost of maintaining loans so small. But mostly it needs enough assets to provide the services it believes are critical for its clients. This means training in handling credit and savings, training in preventive medicine, rudimentary bookkeeping classes and more. Many of these women are illiterate. Some have had two or three years of schooling in childhood. The unbending motivation of many of those women is to make enough money to bring to their children the education they never had in their own childhood. That motivation burns with a religious zeal for most of microcredit's borrowers. Pro Mujer realizes that by staying small it risks becoming more dependent on donor money than it wants to be. That is an institutional hazard in microcredit and the reason why the big accent in the industry today is on "sustainability." It means the lending institution, as a bank or through its banks, is able to leverage enough capital to expand its loans and thus bring in more interest and to keep the revenue stream running deeper.

None of this should be seen has an uninterrupted journey to a land of milk and honey for poor women. The world, after all, runs on "real time" in the language of the political analysts. In many countries of the world, there are still rules of conduct, some prescribed by religion, some by brute tradition. And women are still vulnerable despite the remedies from microcredit.

Helen Todd, the editor of CASHPOR, a network of microfinance institutions that model themselves after Yunus' Grameen Bank, was doing an evaluation of a program in Nepal with a colleague. She tells this story:

> "I was taken to the house of a woman who had borrowed three times from this program…The loans had gone into a grocery business. As soon as I started asking questions, the husband made all the answers . . . Whenever I directed the question at the woman borrower, she had no idea what was going on. The household was doing well. Their income had almost doubled. They had more assets. It was a typical success story.
>
> "Then I followed the woman into the house. When we got there, she started crying. I asked what was wrong. It turned out that her husband, because he had been so successful and

because he was earning money, had taken a second wife, who had been brought into the household just a few months before. The first wife had been shunted downstairs to sleep with the mother-in-law.

"Quite apart from the heartache involved in that situation for the woman client, there is a very strong economic angle. The second wife will have children. Whatever increased income that came from the first wife's loan will be distributed among more people. When I went out, I said to the branch manager, 'do you really think that woman has benefited from the loan?' He got very angry. He could not see there could be a difference between his client's individual interests and those of the household."

In other words, the woman's enterprise here simply fed an ancient culture of male domination and left the woman demeaned.

The story is told here to make a point of reality. The virtues of microcredit have lifted the lives of huge numbers of women. They can't overturn centuries of injustice in one swoop.

But they have overturned much of it. And there are millions of women today from the mountain slopes of Bolivia to the rice paddies of Thailand for whom Catalina Quispe will volunteer as the poster girl. She will do it barging into the market with a hundred pounds of cheese in her cart, a bowler hat on her head and her loan payment in hand.

CHAPTER 7

When Rich People Receive a Priceless Gift

W hen microcredit first arrived in the economic backwaters of the world, the reaction to it among the world's bigtime money handlers was less than white hot.

These were the investment houses, international banks, governmental aid agencies, and multi-million dollar family foundations. To some of them, microcredit looked like a loser. Imagine trying to make bank customers and entrepreneurs out of people living on a dollar a day.

But some of them awoke not long ago to find themselves intrigued by the successes and the prospects of microcredit. More of big capital's money managers, including some who speak for the most prestigious private treasuries and lending-investment institutions in the world, are now seen in the front ranks of microcredit's ardent backers. That support has taken the most persuasive form, in strategies that make millions of dollars in investors and donors' cash available to microcredit pipelines.

Somewhere en route to that seminal shift in attitude, an extraordinary change developed among high-rolling donors. The emotional rewards for them, they discovered, were as powerful as the financial and social rewards for the poor who benefited.

It wasn't an easy conversion. Microcredit was often kissed off derisively as one more save-humanity scheme promoted by some new self-constructed archangel of the poor.

Here is Muhammad Yunus lamenting angrily in Bangladesh that the banking industry's stereotypes of the poor—lazy, uncouth, and a lot less flattering indictments than those—were literally killing the poor:

"Their poverty was not a personal problem due to laziness or lack of intelligence, but a structural one: lack of capital. The existing system made it certain that the poor could not save a penny and could not invest in bettering themselves. Some money-lenders set interest rates as high as 10 percent a month, some 10 percent a week. So no matter how hard these people worked, they would never raise themselves above the subsistence level. What was needed was to link their work to capital to allow them to amass an economic cushion and earn a ready income."

Cynics didn't give that proposition much breathing room. How were impoverished people going to repay those loans, even if they were only for $40, $50, or $100? They were going to take the money and spend it to buy food or clothes, because most of them didn't have enough of either. It was a perfectly normal thing for a poor person to do. And there went the pie-in-the-sky notion of creating millions of mini-capitalists.

But the loans were repaid.

And the borrowers came for another loan. And those were repaid. And the movement spread, attracting new capital from the curious and the generous.

Some of those microfinance institutions, the non-government operations that provided and maintain the loans, went down early. Small loans are expensive to maintain in overhead. The small networks that failed didn't have enough staying power to attract additional money or the economic heft or know-how to recycle their own money by using interest to build reserves.

But Yunus and his replicators showed it could be done. The movement spread. The sound and resourceful networks survived and began to flourish. And the money houses began to see that the big majority of the poor borrowers didn't need a four-year course at Harvard to figure out one of the bedrock principles of capitalism: energy plus opportunity means more. Opportunity meant access to money. Energy meant work and resourcefulness.

More meant a better life.

What people who spoke for millions of dollars in private capital began to see was that there was something going on here beyond the basic charity that most of them practiced as their gesture to the demands of humanitarianism. Most microcredit operations didn't confine their programs and therefore their visions to the simple lending of money.

Most of them put a forced-savings provision into their contract with the borrower. Typically, if you receive a $50 loan to buy fabric or seed for your struggling little business, you're required to (a) pay interest and (b) set aside $5 or $10 in savings that goes into the borrowing group's bank or whatever functions as a bank.

What money experts in Manhattan also saw was that more than 90 percent of the borrowers were repaying their loans. That figure has never been drilled into stone. The one most commonly used is a 95 to 98 percent return, which of course can fluctuate, but it's close, and sometimes it understates the actual repayment rate. Do you want a word that will eventually cross the lips of the average bigtown banker when he sees that number? How about "awesome?"

What became obvious to money handlers as well as social developers was this: Those small borrowers were building their businesses and building their lives, paying off the loan and coming back for another one.

The money gurus saw more. The system gave poor people purchasing power.

It empowered the poor, and especially mothers, to build their own social safety nets.

It provided social and other services, such as basic instruction in disease prevention, infant care, and budgeting and in saving.

It tended to stabilize the political atmosphere in poor societies by building communities of borrowers who shared goals and problems to solve.

It elevated the status of women, and gave an almost sudden new dignity to millions of people who no longer had to grope and suffer for a living or fear for their children.

Increasingly, it paid its way. ACCION and other umbrella groups like it had demonstrated this: that by developing its own banking systems, microcredit was able to recycle and expand money, what Michael Rauenhorst of Deutsche Bank in New York called cranking up the "velocity" of money.

And finally, big capital was impressed by economic pictures like these drawn authoritatively by Women's World Banking:

In the developing (read: "poor") countries, micro or small enterprises made up 80 percent of the total business, more than 50 percent of the urban employment and was indisputably the main source of employment for poor people.

The message was clear. Give those small businesses and poor people a lift, and you would lift the dawdling economies of those countries, make them more livable and in the long run make the world a better and safer place.

Plus—

You were creating new potential customers!

So was it for pragmatic reasons and market-driven reasons that bigger corporate foundations, family foundations, and banking complexes started to get involved with microcredit?

Well, obliquely and only partly. You might argue that they were building future markets and customers by reserving a segment of their office space and clout with investors to promote access to money for poor people around the world.

You might argue that. But it probably wasn't and isn't the primary reason for big capital's involvement in microcredit. The truth is that powerful corporations and banks and corporate foundations reflect the attitudes of most powerful and successful human beings. Unless they are total societal deadbeats out of Dickens' novels, today's managers and custodians of big capital need and usually want to express a humanitarian side. If you want to call it public relations you can. That's part of it. If you want to call it good citizenship demanded by the new sensitivities of our times, you can. It can also, of course, be good business. It gives investors an avenue for their own charitable impulses by setting up plans where investments—say $50,000—to microcredit operations are guaranteed by a corporate foundation like Calvert at modest interest returns.

Money like that made available to microcredit networks in poor countries can expand in a hurry. It produces more capital, more microcredit customers, more self-made jobs, opportunities for families who never dreamed of them, more education for kids, all of that. The money keeps recycling when managed right. And it kept flowing even in the post-boom slump in the American and world economies.

There are some basic paradoxes in the success of microcredit, and ironically, they are critical to understanding why it works. Most of the loans are tiny. But there is nothing flimsy about where much of its support comes from, nor why. The crucial need today is to expand that support, both in the involvement of institutions and foundations and by individuals who see and feel the actual beauty of it in its ethic and its social transformations. The biggest bucks still have to come from governmental agencies.

For a movement that delivers financial service to the poor, microcredit has an impressive array of global powerhouses working to build and sustain it.

You can picture the "cosmos" of microcredit as thousands of loosely connected and often small satellites (MFIs, the working label for Microfinance Institutions) orbiting in a magnetic field held together by some of fixed suns that give it direction, support, and nourishment. Those are permanent international bodies that provide service, money, and networking to the big umbrella groups such as ACCION, FINCA, Women's World Banking, Opportunity International, and many others that funnel money to their affiliates around the world. People who want to learn more about how microcredit operates tend to get impatient or bogged down when they have to plow through the structure. But the big players need to be identified to fill the picture.

Here is **CGAP,** a consortium of 29 donor agencies, mostly the foreign aid arms of 16 governments, including America's USAID. It also includes United Nations' organizations, the World Bank, Inter-American groups, and private institutions such as the Ford Foundation. The mission of CGAP (the Consultative Group to Assist the Poorest) is to improve the ability of those microcredit providers to bring quality financial and training service to the poor—how to bank and save, how credit works—and to do it so that the borrowing group supports itself.

IFAD, the UN's International Fund for Agricultural Development, was set up specifically to combat hunger and rural poverty in the developing countries. Its beneficiaries are the small farmers, the rural landless, nomadic people who depend upon the land, rural poor women, and the poor who depend on fishing. It delivers approximately $450 million annually in grants and loans. Most of that money comes from agencies of the industrial countries.

Another of the CGAP members, the **World Bank Group,** has given nearly $20 billion in loans to more than 100 countries with the idea of bringing new income and new lives to poorest of the poor.

The major U.S. partner in this essentially governmental giving is the United States Agency for International Development, **USAID**. It provides American dollars to countries afflicted by disaster, poverty and famine; and to countries America wants to help or influence politically. It was once a powerful force on the international scene and still performs substantial good. But the changing political winds have shrunk it disgracefully and it now spends less than one half of 1 percent of the federal budget, a figure almost invisible compared with what it once was.

All of these agencies perform valuable services in bettering the health and living conditions of the poor. Unfortunately, because much of that money has been directed to predatory governments, a lot of it has been skimmed by corrupt functionaries and middlemen and wound up in yachts, vaults, and hanging gardens instead of the hands of poor people.

Providers and clients of microcredit are insulated against that kind of thievery. So the dynamic of microcredit isn't something that exits in a novelist's fancy. It's happening.

Some of the principal players in making it happen are the family foundations, patterned roughly after the giant foundations built by families of the industrial tycoons of the nineteenth and twentieth centuries, the Fords, Rockefellers, Carnegies, and on up to Bill Gates' cornucopias of today. Most of them are smaller, of course, but hundreds of them, swollen by the economic boom of the 1990s, annually make grants close to or beyond the million dollar range, a fraction of their total assets. Under law they have to set aside a minimum percentage of their assets for grant making in order to qualify for a tax exemption. Among American foundations, most of those grants obviously are made to non-profit groups or causes in the United States, commonly in localities or regions where the foundation functions.

But family foundations in America come in a vividly mixed bag of interests, passions, and geographic spread. Of the Oswald foundation family members mentioned earlier, for example, one of the Oswald children lives in California, one in Ohio, one in Boston, and the other three in Minnesota. All are adults and voting members of the foundation board. The patriarch, Charley Oswald, maintains an office in Minneapolis and a home and office in Custer, South Dakota. The seven family members meet annually to vote on the proposed grants and awards those grants before the end of the year.

What drives much of the energy in foundation giving is the powerful experience that the act of giving brings to its people, it's familial head and children and their children.

That doesn't mean they will puff themselves up with airy nobility. What it means is that the act of giving, whether it is performed by ladies in white tennis shoes around the Salvation Army kettle or by a man who made millions on cell phones, springs from the same human recognition: "I can give. Here is a need. I can help."

Mike Rauenhorst is a member of a Minnesota family that created several foundations built on the assets of his father, Jerry Rauenhorst, a hugely successful corporate figure in building and real estate, the head of the Opus construction and management companies. Mike works as a consultant for Deutsche Bank in New York, which is active in microcredit. It maintains a $400 million portfolio dedicated to socially motivated loans and investments as part of its community development. Mike talks thoughtfully on what the microcredit movement can mean for both the provider and the borrower:

"What it does for us, I think, is to restore our humanity. In this it has benchmarks. It shows us the value of accountability, how families can work together. It emphasizes openness in how we relate to each other and it expands the dynamics of solidarity. September 11 and its aftermath created many things for us, but one of them was confusion about how to relate to people in need. One of the things we find about charity, straight-out charity, is that it's not simple. It can be complicated. But microfinance simplifies the process of helping. It makes the relationship (between the borrower and the one who makes money available) a partnership. The dollar becomes working capital. You can talk directly to the borrower. The talk doesn't have to be stilted. You talk about real things, like the number of carrots or sewing machines that working capital can produce. You're not talking charity, but a business deal, and both parties see and understand that."

To understand the psychology and emotions of a foundation family coming together to share some of its bounty, the reflections of Julie Oswald offer depth and some enlightenment. They also give us a rare look into how decisions are made in prosperous families committed to giving. Charley Oswald's Foundation was created in the 1990s largely at the urging of his late wife, Sally.

"Our parents taught us the value of independence and following our own path Julie Oswald said. "Our mom had the idea that a foundation deciding how to give money back to society could be a good family project, a way for us to work together. Well, we all rolled our eyes. Why would we want to do that? What did we have in common, professionally, in life styles and in where we lived?"

Julie Oswald is a woman of 41, a teacher of arts to small children and the mother of two. She is a serious but engaging woman who is vitally interested in the changing world around her, in easing the travail of the disadvantaged, in human potential, in art, and in alternative medicines. She admits not immediately being overwhelmed by her mother's suggestion. But she found herself drawn to it after she understood the magnitude of it:

"I remembered one of my sisters saying, 'Gee, Mom. What do you mean finding common values?' We were from different geographic areas and we had different attitudes. One of those attitudes said, 'Gee, dad. It's your money. You decide what to do with it.' Or—'I don't want to get involved in it.' But we talked about it out of respect for mom, and I began to see that it wasn't only a hope of hers, a dying mother, but it had some substance. It had a virtue that went beyond familial bonding. It demanded a commitment not only to be generous but also to be wise.

"We decided to make it an option. You didn't have to get involved if you didn't want to. Personally, I was interested. I didn't know a thing about philanthropy, to tell the truth, but I was open to it. We had an initial meeting and had a range of reactions, but within months of that our mother died. Dad, of course, was supportive of it and eventually got deeply involved in it, but at the time his work was growing successful companies, being in a for-profit world, and being successful. That was his game, and he was good at it.

"When we started forming the foundation, one of the family members decided not to be part of it. The other five said let's go, and eventually the sixth came in. I lived in Minneapolis so I said I'd take the lead. I was an art teacher at the time working with elementary kids and I had two children of my own. We started meeting, and the dynamics were fascinating. We really didn't know which way we were going to do it. How do the eventual grants get chosen (for the hundreds of thousands of dollars the foundation had available)? We had different personalities and obviously different interests. Sometimes it was a struggle. Somebody would make a suggestion for a grant. It would get talked through. There was some defensiveness. It was, 'This is what interests me. Are you going to fund it?' You'd hear, 'Yeah, we will.' All right, great. But sometimes it wasn't great, and there would be an argument. We had to wrestle with how we'd conducted giving in our own lives. Do you just give at the door when somebody comes? Have you ever given more than $100?

"But this was family giving, money we made available in the name of the family, and it was a lot more money, and there were unknowns we had to consider. How relevant was this? What impact will this grant have? How much money do we have to grant to make an impact? Are there better things, more worthy things? Are we being as absolutely responsible as we can? And do we really have agreement here?

The patriarch, Charley, underwent a kind of evolution while the foundation formed. "Dad slowly kept stepping closer to the deliberations," Julie said. "He was a full board member but he wanted to keep hands off while we made the decisions. We said 'you're a member and an active part of this. We need to know what your interests are and share them.'"

And so the family circle filled. It had to develop ground rules. Here was money into the six figures to give away. To whom? How much? About $10,000 here, perhaps $5,000 there, perhaps as high as $50,000. Some heads whirled. The family had money. It wanted to be generous. But those were pretty high stakes for those who got the grants and those who didn't.

"We wanted to develop rules, criteria. To help us, we asked ourselves what did we have in common on issues, urban social issues, shelter, food, and environment? I knew we couldn't please everyone. I was conscious of fingers wagging in my face. It was driving me crazy, trying to create a consensus on every issue. So we decided to advance our own philosophical interests in what we proposed for grant money. For a number of us arts were one, and international needs. That arose from our travel, wanting to see the world and in people exchanges. I lived in France for a time, David, my brother, in Zurich, Switzerland. Others had comparable travel in their life. When my dad worked for the Jostens company in Owatonna, Minnesota, people came from all over the world to visit, and a lot of them were our guests at dinner. So were foreign exchange students. So those were some categories we got involved in. Personal transformation was another, providing resources for the treatment of people with addiction or disorder, lifting people into better lives of self-sufficiency.

"Our mother gets credit for a lot of that. She'd moved us in those directions with her passions and commitments. And we've gotten some of our own children involved to make this multi-generational. They are not voting members of the board, but they understand needs and how to respond to them. We don't have 100 percent enthusiasm on all of the proposals we consider, of course. I think we work most effectively when we can sit down, one on one, and tell each other what it is we like and listen to what the other likes and how we can work together on those ideas.

"In the seven years we've been doing this, I've come to realize this about our family philanthropy: It's just an incredible opportunity to see amazing people doing amazing work. And in that I'm including both those who receive our help and those who create the networks to make the connection between our family and those we want to help. It's absolutely thrilling to see people's visions and how they pull their resources and dreams together, having the vision to address the possibilities no matter how remote they might seem to others, like a small community theater or the whole mission of teaching in Latin America.

"When you look at it that way, it's hard to make a mistake in philanthropy. I think that even if you get into a project that doesn't blossom, you learn from it. You know what to look for the next time. And even if that effort didn't meet expectations, you know you helped somebody who was trying, that you gave that person or those people some hope and momentum. The most exciting part, of course, is when you meet the people to whom you've made a gift, or in the case of microcredit, made possible some of those small loans that have made such a difference in the lives of so many. What feeds us and grows us is this interraction with people who are going down the same road as we are, some as donors, some as the beneficiaries, some as the managers. We're part of a community in a real way.

"To shake hands with them, to laugh and cry with them, that's worth all of the grappling we do and researching and the rest. I once heard David Rockefeller addressing a group about giving. He said philanthropy is finding your heart. That's an ongoing challenge and I'll never forget that. In the visits we've done to the places and people we've supported, I've felt a powerful sense of partnership. If money is what we have to give to bring some light and hope into their world, some satisfactions and dignity and security, then we want to say, 'take it, and let your energies and spirit do the rest.'

That's a great place to be."

Great because it honors both the giver and the receiver.

At 61, an ebullient Sinyati Lebene, the mother of six, has become a poster girl of the new life that microcredit has brought to Maasai women in Tanzania. Once among the most subjugated of African women, they were held down for centuries by tribal codes of male domination. Today Sinyati operates a half dozen small enterprises with loans from the WEDAC and is ready for more.

The shelves are small but immaculate. No dust molests the jars and cans arrayed for her customers by Mariela Angola, who built this successful grocery store in Cali, Colombia with loans from an affiliate of Women's World Banking.

The idea of women in business in Nepal was an alien concept until microcredit began taking hold. Today tens of thousands of women, like these attending a weekly meeting of the organization, Women's Entrepreneurial Association of Nepal, are involved in tiny and growing enterprises. The group's acronym discloses its goal—to wean women in the developing world from the myth that they don't belong in business.

A woman in Samara in Eastern Russia uses her Village Banking plan to rent a stall where she sells fish as a client of a microcredit affiliate of the international FINCA organization headquartered in Washington D.C.

In the mind and the business of Madam Janet in Ghana, there's not much question which comes first, the chicken or the egg. She is the attractive "egg lady" of the neighborhood with an expanding business built with loans obtained from one of the 26 women-led affiliates of Women's World Banking in Africa, Asia, Latin America, North America, Europe and the Middle East.

Their village is a small collection of huts and shacks amid the mud and maize fields of central Kenya. Their parents live below the poverty line. But they're no different from kids the world over. They like to tease strangers when they come into their town of Rwabiti. What's different is that today there is a little pharmacy shop in the village, and it can save their lives.

The little drug store in Rwabiti, Good Samaritan, is one of a network of 27 developed in rural Kenya under a microcredit franchise plan by Scott Hillstrom, a Minneapolis lawyer-businessman whose Sustainable Healthcare Enterprise Foundation has brought medical help to thousands of the poor. It offers low-cost medicines and drugs to

villagers who are vulnerable to childhood diseases. The shop in Rwabiti is operated by three co-owners, who are community health workers and bought the shop with microcredit loans.

Microcredit functions in scores of countries and on all continents of the world in a network of thousands of institutions ranging from smaller ones numbering a few hundred or a few thousand clients to huge organizations in Asia involving millions. Sam Daley-Harris of Washington D.C. is the director of the Microcredit Summit that functions as the international clearinghouse for information, as an advocate in world councils and in the organization of global microcredit conferences.

Nancy Barry, formerly an executive in the World Bank, now heads Women's World Banking, one of the prestigious organizations in global microcredit. It is devoted primarily to freeing poor women and their families from poverty and the advancement women in leadership roles in microcredit business.

PHOTO BY SUSAN WILKES

Martha Umbulla is a familiar figure on the Maasai plain of Tanzania in East Africa, driving the dirt roads in a Land Rover and collecting women for their weekly meetings of WEDAC. This is a microfinance institution of 2,000 Maasai women whose lives have been uplifted with access to money as part of microcredit. Martha is WEDAC's director, conscience, den mother and town crier. With her is a community leader who supports microcredit.

In the mid-1970s, Muhammad Yunus, an economist educated in Bangladesh and the United States, returned to Bangladesh with an idea to reduce the massive poverty in his country and give hope and some working capital to the ambitious poor. He went into his pockets and produced $30 worth of loans to 42 women. Use it, he said, to buy bamboo to make stools and baskets. They did. It was the beginning in Bangladesh of microcredit as we know it today. In the years that followed, Yunus used a simple model: five people, usually women forming a core group of borrowers, then expanding into a larger borrowing and savings group. Eventually this evolved into the Grameen Bank, which became a pillar of the global microcredit movement. Yunus himself became the lead evangelist and catalyst for microcredit around the world—a charismatic man with a simple message to break down centuries of bias and neglect that condemned generations of poor to hopelessness, hunger and pain. Today more than a hundred million people are living better lives because of microcredit. No one is more responsible for that than Muhammad Yunus.

A Tanzanian woman sells fish on the shore of Lake Victoria, one of the commodities she can now bring to market with the credit she receives from a Village Banking loan program of FINCA. She uses the extra income to provide better food, health care and education for her children.

Smiling in the middle of a cornucopia of fresh fruit, a woman of
Columbia fills an order for a customer. This is an open air market
whose sales people include many who have expanded their businesses
with loans from a partner of the international microcredit organization,
Women's World Banking.

PHOTO BY TOM OSWALD

Surrounded by charangos, the popular Bolivian string instsruments,
Martha Lopez Arnez explains her business to American market visitors
in downtown Cochabamba, where competition for charangos is pretty
fierce. Martha sells as well as any. Her husband makes the instrument
but the family wasn't prospering until she got her first loans from
Banco Sol, a business partner of one of the pioneer microcredit institutions in the world, ACCION. As a result, one of their children is now
studying law, another is in psychology and a third is an auditor.

Beatrice Lubega stands before a sign that has become familiar to thousands of HIV-AIDS patients in Kampala, Uganda, identifying the hospital operated for Aids, Widows and Orphans Family Support. Beatrice is its program manager. AWOFS receives support from a variety of non-profit groups, including Trickle Up, McKnight Foundation and others.

Godfrey Mukasa was a wounded soldier in the brutal civils wars that ultimately rescued the people of Uganda from the murderous regimes of Idi Amin and Milton Obote. He returned to civilian life and his family but lost his wife years later to AIDS. A short time later he discovered he, also, was infected. Although he has only a limited time left, this man, scarred by the twin scourges of Uganda, civil war and AIDS, decided to live his remaining years in a way that would give his children a chance in life. He entered a loan program under microcredit, started a small café in his home, toughened himself physically and today is providing a better education for his children. "Life," he said, as one doomed by AIDS, "can be better if you're serving something or someone."

The quickest way to develop new income among poor people with limited opportunities is to invite nature in as a silent partner. Sharda Thapa of Nepal understands this, as well as what goes on in the chicken coop. It's just a matter of time until a few chickens start multiplying and the result is Sharda tending a flock of chicks , which means eggs, and more chicks. And Sharda can thank her first loan from the Women's Entrepneurial Association of Nepal for expanding her business and her family's quality of life.

Flow charts and newspaper accounts chronicle the remarkable progress of the Center for Self-Help Development, begun in Nepal a little more that ten years ago to reduce the historic poverty in that land. It now numbers more than 37,000 borrowers. It's executive director, Mukunda Bista, pictured here, makes the point that while women receive the loans, often they fund a partnership in which the woman and her husband operate a business together or mutually benefit in separate enterprises.

Loans from the Maasai women's microcredit organization, WEDAC, have put Lina Olais of the Meserane group in Tanzania into the jewelry business, both as a producer and marketer. It has enabled her to enroll  her 19-year-old sister in secondary school for the first time and to buy more food and clothing for her three children.

It's not an ivy-covered campus. But apart from food to stave off starvation, schooling is the most important fact of life for developing Africa. This is a primary school for Maasai children in Tanzania. The most devout wish for their parents is that there is something beyond those gnarled logs and crude tables, and that it someday means secondary school and possibly beyond. Microcredit loans and the new income they produce can make that more than a dream. For thousands in Africa, that is happening today.

The weekly meetings of banking solidarity groups are serious business to the ambitious poor in the Third World. This woman is making an application for a new loan at the Uganda Women's Finance Trust in Kampala.

SAVINGS ACCOUNT
PAYING CASHIER

Because banking—taking a loan, making a deposit, saving—is an entirely new world for almost all poor people entering microcredit, the so-called 'Women's Bank" of the Uganda Women's Finance Trust has created a banking atmosphere in its business office, complete with a window where this woman deposits her savings.

Until she discovered the power of microcredit, Jane Nassaka of Kampala in Uganda lacked the barest semblance of self-confidence. She lowered her eyes when she spoke, found excuses to leave when people made efforts to speak to her. Somebody introduced her to a woman's credit meeting. She'd

always aspired to be a hair stylist. She took a loan through a group called UGAFODE, an affiliate of Opportunity International. Within two years she had her own salon. Within a few more years she was styling the hair of customers from all walks in Kampala and, like this one, a visitor from America.

Marketing fruit in a city square in Uganda is usually both a business and a lively social event for these microcredit enterprisers in Kampala.

With profound grief reflected in her face and voice, a woman tells her friends at a microcredit meeting of SEDA, funded by World Vision, of the death of one of her closest friends, a member of the group who was the victim of AIDS. They worked out a plan whereby the group would make up the balance of the loan payment owed by the woman who died. Among the most touching gifts of the microcredit group is the unbreakable bond it creates among its members.

PHOTO BY SUSAN WILKES

WEDAC PHOTO

This woman has just applied for another loan at a weekly meeting of the Maasai women's microcredit group in Monduli, Tanzania. She's beaming because her peers have approved the loan.

Microcredit around the world: Clockwise from the top: Thelma de la Rosa Argote Gomez of San Salvador makes and sells tortillas with loans from El Esfuerzo Village Bank, an affiliate of FINCA. (Photo by Julie Huffaker). Helen Sherpa of Kathmandu, Nepal, directs women's empowerment programs as part of PACT Nepal microcredit. Lutheran Bishop Thomas Laiser is a director of the Maasai women's WEDAC organization, and an affable James Obama manages the respected Pride Tanzania lending and banking programs. *(Photos by Susan Wilkes.)*.

CHAPTER 8

No Mirage:
A Pharmacy Shop in the African Bush

Nairobi, Kenya—

Almost hidden in the banana trees and scraggly bush of central Kenya are a half dozen huts and a muddy little road that make up a settlement called Rwabiti. You can't call it a village. It's not big enough and almost nothing is sold there except—

Except pills for sick kids, malaria tablets, gauze and aspirin, cough syrup and other medicine in small bottles sitting on the spare shelves of a tiny dispensary with no pretense of being a drug store. Call it a kiosk in the brush. It looks a little forlorn but somehow brave. It's crude with its clapboard walls and simple counter, an architecture that resembles what you see in the touring carnivals, the makeshift store-front where hawkers offer stuffed dolls at a dollar for three pitches. But it's clean and straightforward. It seems to announce quietly, "we have medicine. Not much, but we can help."

There is no cashier here. A young man, a church worker, attends it when he can find time from his house calls to give counsel to the sick in his district.

And yet when you come to this obscure place like Rwabiti a few miles from the equator, you come with great respect. There is a difference between this storefront and the scruffy one in the carnival. This one is tidy, and the white paint is fresh.

There's a final difference: It saves lives.

Nothing on the surface connects the kiosk or Rwabiti with a scene several years ago on a lonely rain-soaked highway in New Zealand, where an American lawyer-businessman named Scott

Hillstrom lay bleeding in the night in the wreckage of his car. But the events of the next two hours that night changed the direction of his life and ultimately brought those medicines to the bush in deepest Kenya.

It's a fight just to stay alive in Rwabiti. But there are no throngs at the counter of the little pharmacy shop. Rwabiti is home to 75 people, maybe 100 at most. The ones you see are children. The women are working at home and the men hire out as farm laborers. They will come to the Good Samaritan pharmacy shop a few times a month for discounted drugs they can buy for a few cents. If they have no money, they're not likely to be turned away. Other customers walk miles to get there.

The Good Samaritan pharmacy shop would not be there if Hillstrom had not examined his life while he lay in his mangled car waiting for help.

The saving of lives, the uplifting of millions of people in the poorest parts of the world, is not the province of miracle workers or political potentates. Today's microcredit movement grew from the hard-headed conviction of social entrepreneurs that poor people had dreams and ambitions like anybody else and could be trusted to borrow or manage money; they could be trusted to run plain frame little drug stores buried in banana trees.

Those entrepreneurs come in all races and from all niches in the world's economic fabric, from millionaires to wandering rainmakers with the guts and creativity to pursue an idea. The names of most of them—like Scott Hillstrom, Jonathan Campaigne, Millie Leet, Sam Daley-Harris and Brian Lehnen—appear on nobody's list of global celebrities. Campaigne once hunted for gold and built houses. Millie Robbins Leet was a peacekeeping activist who honeymooned down the Danube to take part in a UN conference on population. Sam Daley-Harris played drums in a symphony. Brian Lehnen was a biologist. You will meet some of these people in Kenya. And why?

The poor and the overwhelmed sometimes have more friends than they realize. Sometimes the hard drivers and swashbuckling achievers of the world, the Type A's, find a way to join the side of the angels and humanity.

The humanity in Africa needs them more than the angels do. Three of those Type As, Campaigne, Hillstrom, and Lehnen, independently took their restless energies and their unblushing idealism into East Africa. Hillstrom and Campaigne began by refining the principles of microcredit and adding an element popularized by some of world's biggest corporations—franchising.

And today as a result, thousands of children in Africa are living healthier lives, and tens of thousands of small business folk are providing decent households and a future for their families.

Hillstrom's entry into the lives of thousands of Africans was something close to an out-of-body experience. He was a man of spiritual depth and corporate success. Yet aside from experiencing the normal compassion toward people in struggle, he had no special interest in actively trying to elevate the lives of anybody beyond his immediate family until that night when he lay alone in his mangled car in New Zealand.

A relaxed life in New Zealand with his family seemed like a reasonable reward for Scott Hillstrom. He was a lawyer and a businessman from Minneapolis, confident and secure after the sale of his company. He was young enough to move in any direction corporately and wealthy enough to be looking for a home for his family in the remote reaches of the Pacific, his Paradise on earth.

That vision was stifled by a rainstorm. Driving a slippery highway in New Zealand after a fishing trip in the mid-90s, he collided with a truck rounding a curve. Both vehicles were destroyed. The truck driver was unhurt. Hillstrom crawled into the rear of his car trying to stem the bleeding from his face. He called to the other driver and asked him to go for help. The nearest city, Queenstown, was 25 miles away. The trucker had to walk and run miles to a telephone on the lonely mountain road, and it would be more than an hour before an ambulance arrived. While it was en route, Hillstrom examined his life. He was drifting toward unconsciousness, in danger of developing hypothermia in the cold New Zealand night. He was fearful of internal bleeding and believed death might be a few minutes away. He thought of summarizing what he had achieved in life: success in career, fulfilling his goals and more. "What I learned was that all the accomplishments, fame, and fortune that life is capable of delivering counted for nothing. Family, friends, God and fellow man were everything. I resolved that if I got through the night . . . I would spend the days God gave me in a better way."

Sometime later in the United States, Scott Hillstrom attended a retreat, read from scriptures, and probed his values. He asked himself what skills he had, what energy he could deliver in finding a better way. While mulling the options, he discovered a startling statistic:

25,000 children die each day, 9 million each year, because they don't have medicine that costs less than a cup of coffee in the States.

He volunteered for some of the larger charities as a resource to make inexpensive drugs available to the poor. Most of those organizations, he grants, perform an acceptable amount of good. But he found some of them were routinely helping pharmaceutical firms to dump drugs into poor countries in order to reap tax and public relations benefits. In Nairobi he met a microbiologist with a Ph.D., Eva Ombaka, who is a recognized world authority on the distribution of essential drugs. This is what she told him:

Between 70 and 90 percent of the death and illness in developing countries is caused by four or five diseases, including malaria and diarrhea. All are treatable with inexpensive, generic drugs. So, he asked, why was it so hard to get life saving medicines to the most vulnerable, the children? The big players in humanitarian aid ought to be able to do that. But most of those today are involved in AIDS education and prevention and in community health development, which are big ticket projects. In the midst of those big programs, Hillstrom found, large numbers of children were dying of diseases like malaria and dysentery. And those lives could have been saved with 50 cents worth of medicine. Further, efforts by some medical organizations to reduce children's diseases sometimes ran afoul of loose management on the ground that made it possible for pharmacy shop operators in the programs to cheat by selling adulterated drugs or peddling drugs on the side.

Hillstrom's solution came right out of the corporate gospels. Put it on a business basis and pull the charity out of it. But how? Walking by a McDonald's restaurant one day, he had the answer. Create pharmacy mini-shops in some of the poorest parts of Kenya, the flagship country, by selling franchises to small partnerships that would include at least one qualified community health worker. He and Eva Ombaka, who became his associate, estimated that a partnership could begin operations with approximately $3,500. That was enough to stock the shelves with essential drugs and medicines purchased at discount rates from reputable dealers in Nairobi and to cover overhead costs and training. The partners would take loans from microcredit donors and sign strict payback agreements covering the three-year life of the loan.

They had to comply with rigid rules of accountability to keep the franchise. And they have. By 2002, two years after the system opened,

27 pharmacy shops were operating in Kenya. Most of them are making it, under the original banner of Cry for the World Foundation. It seemed like a powerful label at the time, pulling at the heartstrings. It has now become a somewhat more dignified Sustainable Healthcare Enterprise Foundation (SHEF), perhaps more attractive to corporate donors. Yet under any name, it's the obscure health workers in the villages who give it value and a quietly powerful message to the poor and their children: they are not alone and will not be abandoned. Because that message is being heard, Hillstrom's foundation was augmented in 2002 by the prestigious Boston-based Management Sciences for Health (MSH). As a result, it now envisions expanding the number of its pharmacy shop clients from the present figure of more than 100,000 a year in Kenya to 3 million people served annually from the nearly 400 outlets it envisions by the year 2006. And it fully expects that entire network to be self-sustaining. An adjunct of MSH, funded by the Bill and Melinda Gates Foundation, will provide technical support for the expansion of those shops and permit the foundation to expand its care and to school its clients in disease prevention and health education.

Those figures are attainable. But they don't hit you in the face when you drive to Rwabiti. To do that you take the main road from Nairobi to Mt. Kenya just south of the equator. After an hour the highway sweeps north and the road to Rwabiti starts plowing into gumbo, passing through fields of maize, small grains and bananas. The coffee growers have moved, denting the meager economy of this part of central Kenya. A few scattered clothes on the lines between huts and three or four kids playing barefoot in the mud tell us that here is Rwabiti. There is practically no commerce. But here is the freshly painted little kiosk, Good Samaritan, belonging to James, Josiah, and Jacob.

On two white shelves are a smattering of medicines: antacids, malaria pills, ascorbic acid, chewable tablets for the common cold, folic acid, tablets for anemia, eyedropper fluid, disinfectant, tablets for heartburn, and aspirin. In a little cabinet next to the shelves is a small collection of adhesive tapes, gauze, surgical scissors, a bedpan, surgical gloves, and a small case of condoms. The three responded to the foundation's offer through their church in a neighboring village. All of them have community health work background, which means they routinely make house calls for their church and now for the pharmacy shop. They tell the women what to do when the children have diarrhea. Not so long ago, thousands of children were dying daily in Africa because their mothers believed the way to stop diarrhea was to withhold fluids.

"They know now that this is not the way," James said. "The information we give is as important as the medicine. We sell what we can to take care of their pain. We can't sell prescription drugs, but many of our customers don't need those. Many of them simply come to us for advice or for things like coughs and stomach disorders that could get worse. About malaria, we tell people to use mosquito nets, and we sell them cheaply; we tell them to cut down bushes and drain standing water where mosquitoes breed. We talk about the need for rehydration when their children are sick, and we talk about the best ways to keep water drinkable."

In the face of the massive health crisis facing most of the world today, what's happening in these little pharmacies in Kenya may seem to be a microscopic response. But one of the most respected public health experts in the world doesn't call it that. Dr. Denis Broun is the former chief of health for UNICEF and is now involved with the Gates Foundation that is assisting Hillstrom's SHEF in Africa. He says this about the bush pharmacies in Kenya:

> "The SHEF shops are so far the only mechanism that have really worked in developing countries to deliver high quality essential drugs to the world's poorest communities in a sustainable manner. Not once, not from time to time...but every day, all the time, through highly motivated private sector franchisees. (SHEF's costs are) a mere pittance compared to the millions of dollars regularly sunk by cooperation agencies and development banks to reorganize central medical stores that benefit far less people."

James Mugo, Jacob Kamau, and Josiah Muchira aren't familiar with the prestige of Dr. Denis Broun or the ambitious schemes of Scott Hillstrom's planners. They are the young investors, partners, in SHEF's Good Samaritan pharmacy shop in Rwabiti, Kenya. They have been at it for two years and they are not getting rich.

But they are saving the lives of kids.

James receives approximately $40 a month for attending the shop daily. The others, investors, receive a token dividend, but none of them has much income, and their lives are pretty much devoted to the health of their villages. That is a commitment. They don't look on it as a sacrifice. In poor African villages, the healthy take care of the others. A small, honest pharmacy is one way. "If they can't pay," James said, "we have something in the budget to take care of them. They trust us. People walk here from several miles away. They know they are getting the medicine that's on the label. We sell or give away condoms and we talk to young people about taking care. We don't preach. But we know we are saving lives, because we know that children have starved here before, or died because there wasn't any medicine, and we don't want to let that happen."

There weren't many customers in the two hours we spent there. But the Good Samaritan performance sheet for 2001 read in part: Cases by diagnosis, malaria 2,809, amoebiasis 232, pneumonia 79, worms 388, pain 201. Just pain. Nothing very special about that, unless you were the one who had the pain. And in this little place in the middle of Africa, someone now cares about that pain.

The deeper your travels take you in Africa and elsewhere into the world's poorest lands, where the need for food, medicine, and friends is the most desperate, the more clearly you grasp a truth about humanity at the turn of the millennium. At a time when words like greed, corporate crookedness, ethnic hatred and pandemic illness are common currency in the languages of the earth, the traveler is struck by another and pretty wondrous side to human nature: the side of service. It is a commitment tens of thousands have embraced. It reveals once more the selflessness of which human beings are capable when confronted by suffering.

This needs to be remembered at a time where our screens are full of angry faces and homeless multitudes, realities that are part of the daily gruel of the earth's news. But there is another reality too powerful and precious to ignore. It comes clothed in all colors and in all ages and all levels of income, skill, and energy. To see it and to be touched by it does not mean you are hopelessly naïve about the real world. There *are* people who care, and care passionately and without regard for the time of day, the season of the year, or the stench of poverty and death.

James, Jacob, and Josiah happen to be Africans, caregivers and dispensers of medicines and therefore life to people only slightly poorer than themselves.

The mix of idealism and tough-shelled skills at solving problems runs deeper among today's young and today's social activists—in all ethnic strains—than some imagine. Halfway across the world is a young American woman, Catherine Inman, from a prosperous family in Minneapolis, walking through the foothills of the Himalayas in Nepal, a place with no roads or electricity, working for The Friends of Dolpa. The need there is for schools, for something that will save an ancient culture, one that originated in Tibet, and do it in a way that will permit the children to retain their identity and to better understand a world around them that no longer ignores them. The Peace Corps legacy is still vibrant. Catherine Inman's work in raising funds for the Dolpans was not directly connected with microcredit. But her commitment to looking beyond herself gives her an unmistakable kinship with James, Jacob, and Josiah, and with Scott Hillstrom. It unites them with a Sam Daley-Harris, a onetime percussion player in the Miami Philharmonic who changed the drumbeat of his life years ago and now directs a Microcredit Summit Campaign, bringing together thousands of people in global gatherings of the movers and visionaries of international microcredit.

So you can multiply these people by more thousands—Americans, Europeans, Latin America, Asians and more. Here in Kenya is a big guy named Brian Lehnen from San Francisco. You look at Lehnen with his bald head and rippling biceps and you're tempted to say, "This guy ought to be a tight end in the National Football League." Sitting at a small breakfast table in Nairobi with his African associates, Lehnen is full of high fives and wall-rattling laughs. This is a gregarious guy, but also a driven guy. He started adult life as a biologist with an MBA in economic development. He was ripe for Silicon Valley in California, and he was going to make it there. But his wife asked him to direct his energies toward human needs in the poor countries. Her idea, he decided, was better. She had experience with World Vision in Costa Rica and the Philippine Islands. With her, he organized a scheme to make $100 grants to the poor in developing countries and called it the Village Enterprise Fund, patterned closely on the Trickle Up model founded by Millie Robbins Leet and the late Glen Leet. These are grants, not loans. They have the virtue of putting money into the hands of people so poor they might not be able to repay and handle the interest on even the small loans that are the staples of microcredit. Millie's scheme was a little different. Make provisional challenge grants. Offer the recipient a $50 grant and a deal: Produce a reasonable business plan, and another $50 grant will follow. It's worked all around the world.

But most grant makers will tell you that they will use whatever system seems right for the culture where they work. In the rural country of Africa, Asia, and other lands bypassed by modernity, most grants are made without strings. For people living in those sparsely populated, often roadless outlands, there is no other way.

Microcredit often can't work there. The loan-maintenance costs of microcredit make it hard for the providers to offer loans to poor farmers. It means travel in the back country, setting up offices there. The overhead is far less costly in urban areas. In developing countries, the poor are vacating the back country in hordes and migrating to the cities, a movement that piles new pressures on the overburdened resources of the cities. Cairo, Mexico City, and Lima are now metropolises of the destitute. But it is the cities that offer the only real hope and sanctuaries for the poor. At least, the poor are convinced of that. The twentieth century phenomenon of the waves of migration to the city is one important reason why microcredit has become first a lifeline and then a passage to new horizons of fulfillment for millions of people trying to battle their way out of poverty.

But unconditional grants do make sense for some who stayed in the backwaters, the rural people. The downside is that since no repayment is asked, the money can theoretically disappear, a one-shot gift that went nowhere. Trickle Up isn't much daunted by that possibility. It finds that people who receive its grants usually make them work to produce more and continuing income. So does Lehnen's Village Enterprise Fund. He explains it:

"We provide $100 grants to 1,200 to 1,400 people each year. Much of our money comes from Silicon Valley in California, and we find that when the venture capitalists there reach the 50s and 60s, they want to put some of their discretionary money into high-impact philanthropy, where it goes directly into the hands of the poor. These are people who want to set up the kind of small business that has a chance. We actually try to identify the poorest of the poor. We maintain a small staff in the United States and in Africa, with 30 volunteer coordinators in each of three countries: Kenya, Tanzania, and Uganda. We consult with people who know the villages in the rural lands, often pastors. We give them a small fee for their services and they help identify the poorest, using standards like how many animals to the people have, the condition of their houses, do they have any money at all, pit toilets, stuff like that. We're talking really poor. We don't use the standard $1 dollar a day income as a measure of poverty. Most of these people have zero dollars. They may do a little work for somebody to bring in a few coins, but it's not much, and they have to eat what they grow. So fundamentally they have nothing and few expectations. But with grants they can get started in something, growing a few more vegetables of their own, setting up roadside stands, selling cane to factories, things like that. A lot of that is done by women."

Which explains why now and then a village woman will smile wryly at one of the volunteer workers when he asks, "how's business?"

"We're richer," she'll say, "than our husbands."

Like anywhere else, wealth in the middle of Africa is all relative. But the presence of Brian Lehnen and his African associates, Jackie Kikuyu, Richard Mazengo, an ordained minister, and Wilson Peru, tramping the roads in rural Kenya, tells you that all of the news in this particular part of Africa isn't bad. Nor is it bad in the hundreds of villages where some form of the International Heifer Project has taken hold—the concept of giving a cow to a family which then gives the ensuing calf to another family, and then more calves and more calves follow. Nor is it bad in the hundreds of farms where American, Canadian, and European industry and nonprofits are making available inexpensive water pumps and grain grinders, linked with microcredit, to create and enhance tiny enterprises that bring new vitality where once there were beaten down lives and apathy.

Is all of this action and new direction of aid money reversing the terrible toll of poverty around the world?

The verdict right now inevitably is mixed. If there has been no sunburst of liberation for the poor around the world, the evidence is indisputable that millions are now living better, more meaningful, and more civil lives. And the biggest contributor to those hopeful strides has been the introduction of microcredit—and the fruitful minds of the Jonathan Campaignes.

Jonathan Campaigne in another age might have been some kind of impulsive good knight, following the sun, sowing ideas, performing deeds, and taking risks. He founded homes for the elderly in Florida, served in the Peace Corps, sifted for gold in Alaska, and finally went back to Africa, looking for a road that would lead him to a mission of significance. He found it in Nairobi, Kenya, after listening to a speech by Muhammad Yunus of Bangladesh, the trailblazer of the modern microcredit phenomenon. Campaigne is now a craggy, slightly rumpled 59, himself a growing legend in microfinance. He knew it had to be Africa for him. "The moment I landed, I felt an electric shock," he said. "It was always in my blood. This was the place where I could do some good. It was a place of welcome and huge need. I wanted to reach big numbers of people who wanted and needed to change their lives."

Campaigne is a humanitarian with the technologue's shrewd eye for the crux of a problem. Microcredit's big problem is making money available to the truly poorest of the poor and cutting down the cost of delivering services. Small loans cost a disproportionate amount of money to maintain. When you lend $75 it costs you just as much in overhead—the bookkeeping and other office maintenance—as though you'd lent $5,000. In microcredit the key to successful lending is the diligence and the good will of the loan officer, who tracks every client as often as once a week, to keep current with the client's needs, health, and performance. So the disparity in cost of loan maintenance is even more lopsided.

Campaigne organized a federation of small loan institutions collectively called Pride Africa. He and his associates made each one of them autonomous. He looked in each case for a leader dynamic, savvy and credible—in Tanzania, James Obama, and in Uganda, Paul Musoke. Both are extroverted high-octane promoters, trained in business and technology. Their client lists run into the tens of thousands, attesting to their perceptivity in picking administrators and their feel for the rub of the road in microcredit. They know the political nuances in their countries and how to move their organizations toward the sacred chalice of microcredit, called sustainability.

That means the lenders no longer have to depend on the moods and choices of their donors. They develop clienteles big enough and successful enough to leverage the money they bank, increasing the sizes of the loans they can make and expanding their rolls of clients. Campaigne moved the five Prides (in Tanzania, Uganda, Kenya, Malawi, and Zambia) in that direction by creating a holding company that provided each branch with network services in software, marketing techniques and administration.

By 2002 their combined clientele totaled more than 110,000, and in some of those countries the parliaments were ready to grant them the status of commercial banks, meaning they could take deposits from the public and therefore expand their products and ability to leverage. Does this matter? "It's crucial," Campaigne said. "You have to look at Africa's cultures to find out what forces can create mass mobilization—aside from the army and religions. We know now that microcredit basically serves the upper edge of the poor who already have a small business, like selling cloth in the market, or selling hot food, or sewing, or selling milk, things like that. The only way we can reach the smallest borrowers and lift them up is to meet their most fundamental needs. And those needs don't include knowing how to manage money. They know that.

"What they need is information. The need to know how money can be available to them, which way can they turn, and what kind of market there is for what they know how to do or are willing to learn. To do that we have to expand our rolls of borrowers, to build systems that can be replicated—in other words, to increase the volume of microcredit so that almost anybody can get it. Then we will have done it and made it a better world for millions who are now left out."

Is that so woolly a dream? No, it's probably not. There is enough money to make it happen. The one true need now is for people who believe that the Campaignes know what they're talking about and that number is growing in Africa.

CHAPTER 9

A Big League Banker
Prowls the Fish Markets

There is something that seems to violate natural law when you put a gung-ho humanitarian in a banking office. It tends to set off alarm bells for the more orthodox bankers and other defenders of the nice, orderly process of making money.

So we'll have to talk to Josias T. DeLaCruz about how and why a manager of the financial empire of a billionaire in the Philippines is now walking around in fish markets and chicken coops asking clients now earning $3 a day how their portfolio is looking. And why he is doing it as the chief executive of one of the newest banks in Manila, literally a bank for the poor, with nearly 20,000 clients and capitalized at nearly $3 million.

One answer to that may be the $3 a day. A few years ago, those people were making less than half of that. Watching microcredit's struggles to make a major, permanent breakthrough as a player in world economics and in the battle against poverty is watching a philosophical tug of war on a global scale. On one side are the microcredit advocates, donors, and practitioners. They have to push the idea, recruit influential and monied allies. They have to do this because they're speaking for millions of chronically impoverished people who already have been empowered with a way to make something of their lives and their families' lives. But how many millions have been left behind?

On the other side are the forces of conventional economics, conventional banking, globalization, and a fair amount of inertia.

Most of these don't normally look like villains, although it depends on who's doing the looking. Globalization wears a lot of garments, and not all of them are pleasing to the eye of advocates of the poor. And you always have to keep your eye on institutional inertia, which is the true lurking dragon for reformers trying to find a way to give decent income to masses of people. About the others, this can be said: In the right ambience and in a world that is fair and filled with good will all around, conventional money lenders and donors wouldn't have to be lobbied and sweet-talked into understanding the zeal and economics of microcredit promoters.

But that is not the world we know. Let's say we accept the idea that an absolute, reachable goal in microcredit is to find enough money in our lifetimes to turn 100 million poor families into small capitalists who pay their loans and their bills. That's the United Nations' goal. Then you have to find a way to ignite the traditional guardians of the rules that govern how banking works. You have to convert them into partners, or at least supporters, of the microcredit movement. The best way to do that is to demonstrate to bankers that microcredit itself is a recognizable, if low-end, part of the banking system. And when microcredit comes into that sanctified lodge, it develops financial muscle. It can do things with money—both its own and borrowed or invested money—that it couldn't before.

When microcredit is in that place, it expands the number of people whose lives it can elevate. And finally it can even turn a profit for the old guard of the banking and investment business who didn't think that possible.

Which is where we meet Josias (Jody) DeLaCruz and Opportunity International.

Opportunity International is a microcredit organization that operates in 25 countries. One of its major vineyards has been the Philippines, where Jody DeLaCruz recently took over as the president and COO of the new commercial bank it now operates in the country. Opportunity International was founded 30 years ago by Al Whittaker, the head of the Bristol-Meyers corporation. It is one of those microcredit fund-raisers and providers that vigorously connect themselves with religious faith. As such, it tends to attract people in this country who have both financial resources and serious commitment to Christianity. Not all of Opportunity International's donors and investment partners are in that category, of course. But among the prime propellants of Opportunity's humanitarian drive is what it calls the spirit and tradition of Christian giving. Not long ago its five lead microcredit institutions or partners in the Philippines agreed to combine their interests and resources. Out of their merger grew the Opportunity Microfinance Bank of the Philippines, on which the Philippine Central Bank has now conferred commercial bank status.

In this it has become one more and a significant trailblazer—along with Grameen, ACCION, and other fundraisers—in broadening microcredit's appeal and prestige in the commercial banking industry. That is the point where a microcredit institution acquires most of the privileges and obligations of a commercial bank. There are others beyond these three, of course, but in the judgment of the microcredit leaders, not nearly enough. More undoubtedly will follow, depending on the government's attitude and policies in the more 100 nations in which microcredit now operates.

The crux of Opportunity International's entrance into commercial banking in several countries is that it can now take deposits, which is the mother lode of banking success. Until it won that approval, its clients who wanted or had to save under the loan agreements often turned over their savings money to free-lance collectors. The system still operates pretty much around the world. Opportunity's Larry Reed tells how it's gone in Ghana in West Africa where Opportunity's partners are involved in microcredit, and why it needs to be changed:

"If you dropped in on a people's market in Ghana, you might see a young man carrying a tin can from stall to stall. At each stall he collects the meager profits from the 'market mamas,' as they're called, the microcredit borrowers, and makes an entry into a small book. After collecting from the vendors, he takes the money to the (commercial) bank and deposits it under his own name. He is one of many *susu* collectors, and they give market vendors a safe, efficient way to save their money. But their services aren't cheap.

"They can charge up to 10 percent a month to collect these funds, and poor entrepreneurs receive no interest on their savings. The only alternative for most vendors is to take the money home, where it might be stolen or spent by other family members."

These small borrowers need a secure place for their savings because they need the money to restock their inventory, and if they can't do that they're out of business. Apart from fees they have to pay to save, they face another penalty. The collector gets the interest their money draws because nowhere are the borrowers identified as the source of the deposits. "They can't borrow against their savings," Reed says, "and their money is loaned to large businesses."

All of which means the normal banking services are not available to the small borrower—unless there's a microcredit bank in the territory that can legally provide those services. After Opportunity Microfinance Bank got its authorization in Manila, which was accompanied by government's power to regulate it, Jody DeLaCruz had a phone call.

"I was working for this billionaire, and the guy on the phone said, Mr. DeLaCruz, can you please become an E-D? I laughed and said, 'What's that?' He said 'executive director.' I asked him what his people did. He said "microfinance." I said I never heard of it." DeLaCruz had an MBA and he was a banker, but he was cipher on the subject of microfinance, a.k.a. microcredit. The man tried to explain. Their plan was to build a bank for the smaller borrowers. "They asked me if I could create a bank. I said I was already running a bank. But I said, 'You'll probably make it worth my while to switch.' This fellow, one of the organization's trustees, said, 'Oh, Mr. DeLaCruz, we can't afford to pay you what you're getting now.'

"I said, 'Wait a minute. I'm running a bank and six real estate companies for this billionaire and you want me to do harder work at a lot less pay.' The guy said yes. I told him they did noble work but I was comfortable where I was. Two weeks later these people called again. I said I'd made my decision. They said they'd prayed for me and then they asked *me* to pray about it, because I was the person they wanted. I said that wasn't quite fair because if I didn't take the job it looked like I had a swelled head and I was probably going to get hit by lightning. But I did pray about it. After a while I thought this: Here was a group where I could be a Christian for seven days a week, where I could finally find fulfillment in what I was doing, and where all my experience could fall into place in behalf of people in need."

It didn't hurt the petitioners' cause that Jodie had been born in a shanty, that when his mother was carrying him she had to walk down three flights of unlit stairs at night to use an outdoor toilet that his family shared with 12 other families. But his parents never wavered in their search for a place in the world that would reward their energy and commitment. His father became a surgeon, his mother a banker. Jody studied in the states and later in prestigious Asian schools. By now he was soaring in private commerce, drawing big money at 41, married and the parent of three foster children.

But not long afterward he was running and hustling a microcredit bank with fish pond and chicken coop people as his customers.

"But it became heady stuff," he said. "Without their own commercial bank, microcredit operators could make loans, but they couldn't set up shop and tell the world, 'Okay, boys, come in and make your deposits.' Deposits are the cheapest source of income for a nongovernmental operation. So the now the deposits were coming in and could be leveraged to bring in more money, and those deposits would be insured by a federal institution.

"The leverage business is a big deal. It meant that now you had a formal institution in microcredit, and other banks could lend you money several times the size of your capital. Another bank could say, 'All right, you have a million dollars in capital. We can now lend you five times your assets. And right there you're in business, with a lot of ways to go with your new resources, especially in building up more loans, bringing more chronically poor into the system, drawing interest on those expanded loans . . ." Thereby reducing the per capita overhead costs of maintaining those loans.

And what he saw in the bank was a revelation that had the onetime barefoot kid from the shanty gulping in thanksgiving and pride.

"A majority of these people had never been to a bank before," he said. "What we were doing was inviting them to come into a bank for the first time, for leases, for loans. Many of them had never seen a check in their lives. Many of them burst into tears when they did. They said they had never been entrusted with so much money, small as it was in our eyes. I'm telling you, this is one of the most exciting things that's happened in Asian banking: Five microcredit operations merging themselves into one bank, institutions that until then couldn't take in deposits, couldn't leverage money, were in effect pretty much doomed to stay small."

And all the while the new commercial bank of the small borrowers was urging them to learn how to save. And why was that hard to do? Jody explains:

"The Philippines are notorious for having one of the lowest savings rates in Asia. People aren't conditioned to it. They just have never been big for saving money for a rainy day. If they had any extra cash, it went for the fiestas. They even borrowed for that. That tradition was even more damaging to the poor. They couldn't send their kids to school or the hospital. If they had somebody in the family with an addiction, they had to dig into the food money.

"So we bore down on changing that pattern. And the reason the government was willing to authorize Opportunity Microfinance as a commercial bank was pretty much a desperation thing. Nothing else in the battle against poverty has worked. Local governments used to give small loans but didn't have the money to monitor the loans. Charity doesn't go very far. Politicians made handouts, but that was a dead end, too. The problems for government have gotten worse. Terrorism has been around in the Philippines now for some time. Bin Laden had a connection there. But whether the terrorism came from an Islamic or other group, mostly it got down to banditry. They were terrorizing, kidnapping, to extort money."

Globalization, despite some of its virtues, hasn't especially helped the poor in many lands, of course. Globalization puts a premium on big, competent, multi-national companies. The losers when it becomes a contest are the little businesses. In the Philippines, it's cheaper for families in a lot of places to buy imported fruit rather than home-grown fruit.

So with Jody DeLaCruz, you have the symbiosis of hardheaded banking savvy with the passions of a man who grew up in poverty. He knows its grip and its terrible fears. And because he does, he now finds himself able to use his skills and both his love of his people and an understanding of their traumas to bring them into a life that offers them a pride of achievement that was denied them from birth.

Those qualities, running on parallel tracks, characterize the builders of the microcredit movement. And the appeal of the movement is that financiers and humanitarians alike in the most prosperous countries have leaped into that tug of war on the side of microcredit.

The game is a long way from a culmination. And the stakes are enormous: better lives, healthier lives, and more meaningful lives for millions of families. And, perhaps, peace.

CHAPTER 10

The Loan Manager
Who Survived Idi Amin

Kampala, Uganda—

Political moralists in the West work themselves to the brink of apoplexy in their fervor to denounce the horrors of corruption in Africa.

The solutions are endless: Stop pouring money down the rathole. Make them swear an oath on top of Kilimanjaro that they're going to adopt democracy, free markets, and cafe lattes at Starbucks before they get a dime.

Swithern Tumwimne has heard most of the solutions and sympathizes. He is probably wiser about African corruption than the moralists and may deserve a wider audience. Swithern is a manager of money in Uganda. He does this in a workplace that has the uncorrupted ability to bring food and clothes into the homes of thousands of families and does. He is a man of patience and insight into the roots and pain of poverty, a big-shouldered man with a quiet but authoritative voice and a history that generates instant respect among those who work with him. When he was young, he heard the sounds of firing squads in his village, a place ripped by the ferocity of civil war. He survived to receive an education and to become a supervisor of microcredit in Kampala.

He is embarrassed by the culture of theft, bribery, and miscellaneous profiteering that are generic among governmental and corporate hierarchs and bagmen in Africa and in poor countries around the world.

He believes this: The theft of money intended for the public can be slowed, and sometime in a future millennium, eventually stopped by the same kind of people who now are building their lives with the small loans of microcredit.

Tumwimne is no theologian nor economist. He manages small loans given to thousands of the poor. But his rise as a voice of conscience and integrity in the lending industry deserves attention. In his own country, he has seen the abuse of power at its tyrannical and murderous worst, corruption at its most larcenous. His family might have been its victims. It was at the time of civil war in Uganda during the slaughters that bloodied the rainforests in the regimes of Idi Amin and Milton Obote. Tumwimne's family got through it, and after the wars sent him to school to learn business. His presence and character mark him as a leader. He thinks he knows how reform can come in countries where corruption has turned government into an institutionalized racket.

The intentions of the western reformers are good. The history of their strategy isn't. The popular axiom of the today is to set up a formula: "We'll give you the money only if you show us something good we can see. Move toward democratic government. If you can't do that, you're not worth the risk."

It's a quid pro quo that makes sense to most Americans, with their reverence for the democratic system. And more progress has been made toward democracy in some of those the African countries than might reasonably have been expected, considering the shambles left by the departing colonial powers in the twentieth century. But political reform of Africa's struggling poor countries, only a generation or two removed from the straitjacket of colonial exploitation, is not going to come as a thunderbolt in the night. The eventual heroes of reform in Africa are far more likely to be people who were born there and have survived the kind of life-and-death crises most Americans could not imagine.

The reformers-to-be are Africans like Swithern Tumwimne and their clients, the thousands of obscure small enterprisers in Africa's cities and villages who have pulled themselves up with honest commitments to build a business and trust in their partners. Because they have, and because the fledging democratic movement in Africa eventually has to gain significant ground, they will insist on seeing the same quality in their politicians.

In the pragmatic mind of the foreign aid money cruncher in America and Europe, that sounds naïve and visionary. Well, it *is* visionary. Swithern Tumwimne was not talking about tomorrow or next year. He was talking about a long, slow climb, which is what the realistic prospect is for a functioning if imperfect democracy in the developing countries of the world.

But on that point, we might give ourselves a kick in the shins to guard against easy smugness. Democracy in what we like to call the world's greatest democracy hasn't always been dependable and honest. In fact, it isn't uniformly dependable and honest today, nor—as we have seen—have been the money handlers in some of the biggest corporations in America.

So we can check our piety at the door of the thatched huts in Africa. Swithern Tumwimne knows about deep corruption and graft in the African countries, which have long been part of the governmental and corporate schemes in countries of poverty. He thinks the performance of microcredit in Africa can reduce it and eventually expose it often enough to make a difference until a real and authoritative democracy takes hold. This is Swithern Tumwimne's belief as a man who grew up witnessing murder by military thugs in his village and who brought into his own family the orphans of a brother who died of AIDS. He now directs a program in which mounting numbers of Africa's poor, predominately women, have transformed credit into new and productive lives. "That is empowerment," Swithern said. "It also tells people what honesty means in handling money. It has given them some control some over their lives. When they see people in government mishandling money, they're not going elect those people."

That's still a long way from being a surging, popular tidal wave demanding honesty in government. The political atmosphere in most African countries is not conducive to popular demands. But there is clearly a rising new conscience of the people in many of those countries, growing out of their small but measurable triumphs in the marketplace. Swithern is one of their leaders and advocates. His personal history, the threat of death in it, is a snapshot of the life in the gruesome civil wars of Africa.

When Swithern was a boy he saw the death squads of Idi Amin in his village, killing men and women suspected of being sympathetic to Amin's opposition:

> "We'd find bodies in the nearby swamps. It was a terrible life, not knowing if we would be next. It was not much different later in the Milton Obote years. My father was an enterprising man who was a successful farmer. He was a leader of the village and a Christian. There were people in the vil-

lage jealous of his success. There were whispers when the soldiers of the Obote regime came. My father was arrested. They thought he had a gun and they tried to force him to admit it. My father said he didn't have a gun and they could search and not find one. They took him into the woods. Our family was terrified. We followed them and heard gunshot. We waited. We thought he was dead.

"But he came walking out the woods. He said they kept asking him where was the gun. He said, "I don't have one. You can kill me, but I don't have a gun." They told him to say his prayers. Then they shot in the air and let him go."

These were killing fields that in their youth had become the daily environment for many of Africa's executives of today, women as well as men. In America, management leaders decorate their walls with MBA certificates and the credentials of three or four universities. In their pockets are the keys to an Audi, parked in the covered ramp. In Africa the management leaders tend to make a lot of funerals. But their walls are decorated with the photos of women with the irrepressible smiles of people who have broken through their faceless existence of before. That was a time before they learned they could borrow money, pay it back, pay the interest and sell more baskets and bake more pastries than they ever did because they could now *buy* more to sell.

Is this a sexist, condescending picture of women and the enterprises open to them in Africa as well as most of the developing world?

It is not. It's life in Africa today and in most of the poor countries on earth. And for these women, it's a beginning. We can't measure their possibilities and their ambitions by what's available to American women. An American woman will land a place on a corporate board or get a coaching job or drive an eighteen-wheeler or a 747 jet. For every American who scores these achievements, there are thousands of women around the world who break through into another life and another world of achievement by borrowing $75, paying it back, and putting up clothes on rack in an outdoor market.

Swithern was 17 at the time of the incident involving his father in the 1980s. The family had enough resources to send him to college. With the onset of the Museveni government in 1986, Uganda began to stabilize. Swithern learned about microcredit. He became an executive in it in 1997. His zeal to make life better in Africa is expressed in pensive and almost meditational tones. But it is a commitment that is unmistakable. He knows, though, that it is foolish to let his ideals loosen his hold on reality in Africa going into a new century.

Reality is that people in Africa have been dying faster than almost anywhere in the world. Reality is that much of Africa is run by militarists or entrenched autocrats who don't like to open the gate to opposition parties. But he knows that can change, and, in his Uganda, it *is* being changed.

Swithern is one in a growing cadre of African social and economic trailblazers. Their clients are part of the worldwide millions who today are capitalizing on those small loans to bring new money and expanded lives to their families and into the futures of their children. The leaders in this system are aggressive young men and women, trained in business, who are driven by their personal experience with the monumental grief of Africa in the last 40 years. It gives them a goad to service and to liberate their people from poverty.

Although by American scales it's microscopic banking, Uganda is a whirlwind of microcredit action. It's part of a national mentality to move past the horrors of its civil wars and AIDS and to do it without pleading (at least not round-the-clock pleading) for western economic wizards to come to the rescue. "Those things (the wars and AIDS,)" said Janet Museveni, the wife of Uganda's current president, "did not break our spirit. Our people are determined to survive." The Ugandan president, Yoweri Museveni, is more progressive than most of the African strongmen who emerged as long-term leaders. He is still shy about multi-party elections, but despite the continued threats of insurgents along the Sudanese border and in pockets elsewhere, Uganda strikes the visitor as a country charged with energy, willing to risk new ideas and hungry to create a new solidarity. On billboards in the capital city of Kampala are graphics that endorse a pragmatic way to reduce the threat of AIDS. "No glove," the message declares in three-foot letters, "no love."

It's saucy and it has its critics. But conversation in Uganda is freewheeling and open, and that message is hard to ignore. So is the passionate movement toward solidarity, Ugandans doing things together. It evolved from the desperate need to feed, shelter and embrace into new families the multitudes of children orphaned by AIDS. Their number runs into the millions. Thousands of volunteers responded to a call by Janet Museveni, including a woman who has become a kind of national heroine, Nakayima, a 70-year-old grandmother of Masaka.

All eight of her adult children died of AIDS.

All of their spouses died of AIDS.

They left 35 children. All of them are now cared for by Nakayima, their grandmother, in a house built by the friends of the Uganda Women's Effort to Save Orphans, UWESO, which was founded by Janet Museveni. The Ugandan citizens' spontaneous rally to the victims of AIDS and to their orphans is one of the compelling stories out of Africa, or out of anywhere, today. So is the spirit of the country, whose wild nature is one of the most spectacular in the world with its Lake Victoria, its source of the Nile, its Ruwenzori Mountains of the Moon, Murchison Falls, and gorilla lands. And AIDS is coming down. Nearly a third of the population was infected not long ago. The figure is now below 10 percent.

The spirit of it is reflected in one of the weekly meetings of the borrowers under microcredit. The sounds you hear there may be the preludes to genuine democracy in Africa.

Take a moment to sit at one of the tables, as Susan and I did. The borrowers meet once a week. They were much too occupied with numbers and deadlines and new loans to be distracted by two visitors who were fascinated by the raw energy surrounding them. The clients were brought together by their elected board. This was no stockholder meeting. It was part country auction and part revival rally. You should first have a working definition of the kind of small business that brings bread and milk to small borrowers like these, who dwell mostly at the poverty line. When small business is mentioned, most Americans first exposed to the idea of microcredit have a tendency to think in terms of American small business. That means a music shop, a row of storage units, a family-operated motel, a consignment store, or a body and fender shop.

It's not what small business is in Africa or in most developing companies. Swithern is the executive director of an African-originated microcredit group called UGAFODE (Uganda For Development). He runs through the catalogue of small business sustained by $50 to $100 loans in Uganda. "People sell fish that they net in Lake Victoria; they sell Irish potatoes and bananas in the market; they make saucepans and kettles. Some of them fatten bulls or sell a half dozen groceries, or they sew or sell cloth. When the tourists come, you see some of them selling woven baskets. You also see people shining shoes. It's very small stuff. But they work long hours, and they work almost every day."

On this day they were meeting to make the weekly payments on their loans and to apply for new ones. Small currency, handwritten status reports and some creative giggling filled the hall. It was African sponteneity at its most vivid. There weren't many wallflowers in this bunch. Nearly 95 percent of them were women, some of them in their church and wedding best, others in skirts and sweaters. The treasurer, the resident beancounter, piled stacks of shillings on a battered table top in front of the assembled borrowers, sitting in rows of folding chairs. A bill fell off the stack and five outstretched hands came out of front row to rescue it before it hit the ground. These folks tend to respect money. Each client came armed with a passbook and a plain paper journal of figures. This was not Palm Pilot sophistication. But it wasn't count-on-your-toes stuff, either. The clients knew their arithmetic and what they could handle in interest and set-asides for savings.

Loud voices competed for attention on the floor, and other voices murmured so only one set of ears could hear. It was a show, because nobody does meetings quite like Africans do. When African small loan clients gather, you see theater, business, some impromptu shake-and-baking, and a lot of unbuttoned laughter. Some of them talked to their loan officers in low and confidential tones, but it may have been nothing more serious than what you hear at the water fountain. The loan officers are ubiquitous. They roamed the meeting hall with advice, handshakes, and some squirms of anxiety. Later in the week they would be visiting the borrowers and keeping tabs and telling them they were doing well or doing a great job of catching up. Nothing much escapes the loan officers in microcredit. They are its wardens and the money counters and the rough-cobbled guardian angels of microcredit. At the meeting, the borrowers voted on a loan application by a woman who had once failed to make a payment. The loan carried. Applause. The applicant was trustworthy. When she had fallen behind, her friends put her account in balance by volunteering their own money, which she repaid. When the meeting ended, they all locked arms and sang a solidarity song.

These are people who are still scraping to get by, but they now are scraping *after* buying clothes for the children and putting a little more food in the house. Microscopic loans don't mean microscopic interest payments. They have to make those payments at a rate of 20 to 30 percent because it costs the providers to maintain small loans. But for the first time, those people are saving something in the bank and planning for the biggest of all days—when their kids can go to secondary school and maybe then to college. They now enter each day with belief in themselves and trust in those who share their meetings.

"They can do those things now," Swithern said. "They couldn't before. The organization they belong to, our organization, UGAFODE, is African from the start. There are a lot of microcredit institutions that were located here in Africa through the work of donors and agencies in Europe and the United States. And for that we're thankful. But this one was started here by an African evangelist and was set up as the African Evangelistic Enterprise. It later found an advocate in Opportunity International in America, and we now have 8,000 clients receiving credit and saving and expanding their small business. We've reached the point where we're 90 percent sustainable (meaning UGAFODE can finance its loans and maintain its training and educational services almost without donor assistance—but not quite)."

There is passion in these people. It's in their eyes and the intimacy with which they greet each other. They have found something. There is passionate thankfulness in the eyes of Jane Nassaka, in her little hair styling salon on the edge of Kampala. She is a classically beautiful young woman who before discovering that she could trust people, before discovering that she had worth, could scarcely talk. She couldn't make eye contact, could not imagine herself as someone who mattered. Today she handles 10 to 15 customers a day, banters with all of them, and has a dozen friends. It began with a $50 loan. She paid it off. She took another. She acquired confidence in who and what she was. And for a struggling Africa, she is one who matters very much.

CHAPTER 11

"I Feel Your Pain and Share Your Dream"

Author's Note:

Susan and I returned from Africa in the spring of 2002 with images that would not quickly be erased during the usual adjustment to America's pace and energy. Some of our memories were profoundly disturbing, others inspiring in what they told of the will of a people, all but abandoned, to overcome and to live. We talked about the AIDS hospital in Uganda, the men and women sitting stoically on the benches outside the entry, waiting for medicine, but more: waiting for the embrace of someone who understood their need for acceptance and love.

That scene and many like it from the impoverished countries of our most recent visits exerted an emotional power that moved Susan to remember them not so much as a longtime manager in human development, but rather as an American woman and mother. Inevitably she found herself comparing what she had just seen and felt in Africa with the opportunities, comforts, and choices of her own life in America. For these she feels more than gratitude. What she feels is an urgent summons to solidarity with the poor women she met and to expand the community of giving, a community united in the simple declaration: We can help.

I asked her to put down those reflections because they are important for an understanding of the purpose of this book, to draw attention to the power of microcredit to create better lives for millions. Her thoughts are vivid, personal, and they matter.

Jim Klobuchar

Susan writes:

The front-page headline in a newspaper reads: "Hunger Stalks Southern Africa." It is the first in a four part series on a "Continent in

Crisis."

I have read this before.

Inside there is a double page spread: children with huge eyes, distended stomachs, sticks for arms and legs; exhausted and hopeless mothers; four listless children sitting by their mother, who is trying to suckle a baby, sharing a bowl of fortified cornmeal at a nutritional rehabilitation unit in the Dedza region of Malawi.

I have seen this before.

I read the article. Half of Zimbabwe's 12 million people are in dire need of food. Three million in Zambia face starvation. The list goes on and on.

I cringe. I see the list of international food-aid agencies to which I could send money, but I think my money is a drop in the bucket. Even humanitarian agencies can't keep up with the crisis.

How rarely do our media cover these disasters in the making. When they do, I watch my friends and neighbors slowly tune out. They are not callous, but they think it's hopeless and there's nothing one person can do.

I think, this happens year after year. Why? What can I do? What can we do, living in the richest country in the world?

There have been other headlines: "Terrorism on the rise," "Hunt for bomb plotters," "U.N. inspectors ready to roll," terrorism, terrorism, terrorism.

Don't we see the connection?

I think about my own three beloved children. What would it be like to gradually watch my children starve to death? What would it be like to know that even if they lived, abject poverty, war, disease, despair, would be their lot? Would I have to sell my body to feed them? Would my daughter have to sell hers? Would I bring HIV/AIDS into the family? Would I sell a child to a rich family so that he or she might eat? Would I follow some of my more desperate sisters and maim a child to wring more pity and coins from a tourist, just to keep the other children alive? How would I choose which one? If they survived, would they have any hope of schooling? Of a job? Of a life?

I know my sons: They would fight being condemned to such a future.

How would they fight? Who are the foot soldiers of the fanatics? They are sons like mine, if my sons were desperate and angry. Young men who feel ignored and abandoned will follow a leader bent on revenge for colonialism. They will resent the wealth and callousness of the industrialized world, resent Americans unwilling to share their bounty because they have turned their eyes away or they are too busy with their own lives, making money, watching football games, shopping for the holidays, enjoying the good life.

I see another headline: "Why do they hate us?"

There are many causes of terrorism, but conditions of hunger, poverty, indignity and hopelessness are breeding ground for much of it.

What can we do? What can I do?

I am a mother. I am a Harvard educated professional with a husband whom I adore, a big house we've made a home, books to read, and food on the table everyday. I have a good life. But my conscience won't let me sleep when I read about the plight of millions of families, fathers, mothers, children around the world. The last time I came home from Nepal and Tibet, I could hardly bear to go to our grocery store, overflowing with every kind of food imaginable while people are starving.

I am worried. I am worried about the future for my children. Will we share our wealth before we are forced to do it by violence and revolution? Will we see in time that the destitute of the world are human beings, mothers like me, children like mine, with the same hopes and aspirations that have been the drivers in my life? They yearn to be acknowledged as human beings with rights: to be heard; to vote; to have unquestioned access to food, clothing and shelter; to be free to choose their own paths, jobs, sexual customs; to use their own talents and energies to care for their families, participate in the lives of their communities and countries and live in peace with the human family.

Years of international travel, teachers, colleagues and friends on every continent, plus my own innate optimism and my international education and development work have led me to a compelling answer to "What can I do? What can we do?"

Nineteen years ago I created a model statewide center for international education, foreign languages, exchange, and economic development in Arkansas. Shortly thereafter the Winthrop Rockefeller Foundation and Bill and Hillary Clinton became interested in Mohammad Yunus's vision of banking for the poor. With them, I learned about microcredit.

I was absolutely fascinated by the simplicity of the idea, its potential to transform the lives of millions of people, its record of effectiveness even then, and the passion of its founder. I met people from Southshore Bank in Chicago, who had successfully translated the method into programs in the inner city there. I became part of an effort to try it in rural America, in Arkadelphia, Arkansas. I have been an advocate and supporter ever since.

Before that time and since I have traveled and worked individually and with my husband Jim in Africa, Asia, and Latin America. We have seen up close and talked with emaciated mothers with babes in arms begging in the streets of Kathmandu, children maimed by their families to elicit more coins from passers-by in Rio de Janeiro, families on the edge of starvation in Tanzania or decimated by HIV/AIDS in Zimbabwe, 15 year-old orphans of AIDS struggling against terrible odds to provide for their younger siblings in Uganda. I know that the newspaper photos I see, the headlines I read, the chilling briefings I receive through my international work are *real*. I am not cushioned by distance, second hand information, or a television screen. I must do something.

I know that Jim and I have found a way to impact these terrible conditions that so deeply concern us. The gateway is microcredit. As you have seen it described in this book, microcredit multiplied many times is the single most effective and rapid way an individual, a foundation or a corporation can help these desperate people work their way out of poverty. The stories you read in this book are recur in countries all over the world, whatever their political condition or system of government.

Microcredit, well done and well supported, gives hopeless mothers, fathers, and families a chance. They love their children as we do and would do anything to save them and give them a future. Mothers, with a little help in the form of very small loans, develop little businesses that put food in their children's stomachs, medicines in their reach, schooling in their lives and hope in their hearts.

Many people take the position that it's hopeless, that we can only help one person at a time, and that takes forever. Through village banks and their counterparts, microcredit helps 35 to 50 women at a time, which means 250 or more members of their families. Multiplied by thousands of such groups and thousands of microcredit institutions across the globe, it means millions. With more funding support from rich countries and from rich-by-comparison people, change for the poverty-stricken could skyrocket!

There are striking by-products: the empowerment of women to stand up for themselves, develop and own their own work, provide for their families, control access to their bodies, contribute to their communities, and often emerge as leaders. Many microcredit programs emphasize literacy for women, giving them the power that comes with information. That in turn gives them a heightened sense of identity and self-worth that comes with writing their own names instead of a thumbprint.

Health and nutrition conditions improve in every family involved in microcredit. Imagine changing the health conditions and budget of a village, city, or country from the bottom up!

I believe that building a foundation for democracy is another by-product: Thomas Jefferson wrote that an educated populace is essential for democracy to flourish. Microcredit can begin the process of education for poor children, their mothers and their families. Over time they will read, begin to ask questions, advocate community and national change, and become informed voters.

Microcredit can be effective in halting the AIDS epidemic currently ravaging the African continent, soon to be as or more devastating in China and South Asia. With economic power and health education, women can say no. Women can build income-producing businesses, selling vegetables instead of their bodies. Men can join their women working in the villages instead of seeking work in the cities and bringing home AIDS.

Microcredit relates to local security as well. AIDS is decimating the military forces of many African countries. Education, alternative jobs, wives with small businesses can help reverse this trend.

Microcredit can help protect wild animals and precious lands: the Jane Goodall Institute uses microcredit in Eastern Tanzania to provide food and income alternatives to killing chimps. In rural Nepal, women learn new agricultural techniques that prevent deforestation, as their small loans bring them training and information about alternative crops and marketing techniques.

Microcredit can touch and improve almost any aspect of life in poor countries. Does corruption discourage you from funding projects in these countries? The microcredit institutions, large and small, that we have visited, are run by young, smart, educated, and committed indigenous men and women, often MBAs, who direct financial operations so dispersed, involving so many loan officers and self-organized borrower groups that their transparency is inevitable. Could these men and women be modeling for their countries financial services that are free of corruption?

Today I advise and manage family foundations. I have introduced many to the miracle of microcredit and taken family members to visit programs that they have funded. When they meet women who are running their own small businesses and hear about the impact on their families and on their own sense of self-worth, these Americans are stunned. Their view of the poor in the developing world is radically revised. They see proud and smart entrepreneurs, capitalists if you will, pulling themselves up by their own efforts. Their launching pad was a small grant, equivalent to the cost of a haircut here, less than the cost of an opera or professional football ticket, an amount each of us could easily do without. It's the American way, they say, and it works!

My class at Radcliffe was the first in which the women received Harvard degrees. Our reunions are with the Harvard men. We often talk about the condition of women then. We were right on the edge of the women's revolution, many of us with no goal other than to be married, others with high ambitions. We have watched the world change for women in this country. We ourselves have experienced the battles and the triumphs and watched as our daughters move into a world very different from ours.

I often think, what if women in this country decided to change the world for women everywhere? What if we claimed solidarity with our sisters in developing countries and made it our goal to see that everyone of them has an opportunity to lift herself and her family out of abject poverty and despair?

Could we do it? Absolutely. We changed the world for ourselves and we can do it for them. All we need is the will and the right tools. Microcredit is one of the tools and we can all get behind it. We can talk about it—it is not well known in this country—and we can share our income and our capital with these women through microcredit institutions.

My family has a small foundation in Buffalo, New York, created by my great uncle, who was father of Katharine Cornell, the extraordinary actress of the first half of the twentieth century. Until I became a trustee, it had not given an international grant in 50 years of philanthropy. We know that needs in Western New York are great, but today we give a percentage of our grants to microcredit groups in developing countries. We do so because we know that even a small amount of money goes a very long way there and radically improves many lives. We see that the money is leveraged many times over. And we know that we are making our own world a little safer by helping to reduce the inequalities in the world.

We make a point of giving grants that undergird the delivery systems of microcredit. Families and individuals get great satisfaction from knowing that their gifts go directly to the mother or the family, and rightly so. But we also need to support the people and systems that make small loans possible, the loan officers, the motorcycles that carry loan funds to remote rural areas and bring back savings, the technology that keeps track of thousands of tiny loans and helps cut the costs of serving millions.

I am not talking about charity. I am talking about investment in microcredit groups and loans that are repaid 95 percent worldwide. I am talking about investment in the security of our families and America. I am talking about investment in stability and peace in the world. I am talking about American individualism and a banking idea that gives every woman participant the right to be seen as an individual, a human being, and a member of the human family.

After September 11, we in the United States were suddenly face to face with the world. Far more of us than ever before tried to learn about the world, the political and religious issues, the conditions of inequality that divide us. Some of us reacted with fear, but many of us wanted to know what an individual (or a foundation or a business) could do to help turn around the dangerous situation in which we found ourselves.

We Americans are generous by nature and at our best, good at sharing with those less fortunate than we. We poured out our hearts and our pocketbooks to help the victims and the volunteers in New York. But we didn't find a good answer to the question: what can we do to change world conditions so that terrorism does not become the inevitable future for all of us?

I believe that a massive effort to support the microcredit movement would do more than anything else we can do personally or institutionally to alter the enormous inequalities in the world and the resentments they breed. We can't wait for government-to-government programs, which often do not work anyway. We can support right broad grassroots change in partnership with the ambitious poor by providing loans that allow them to help themselves.

Microcredit is not an experiment. Its record of achievement runs to more than 30 years in length and millions of people deep. It is sanitized from government corruption. Its repayment rate is astonishing. It works. It's here and it needs now only to grow.

CHAPTER 12

A Muslim Woman Builds a Factory on Christian Trust

C airo, Egypt—

In the 5,000-year history of the women of Egypt, the name of Samya Abd Aelazeem is no match for the candlepower of the luminous queens Hatshepsut, Nefertiti, and Cleopatra.

Hatshepsut's glory is enshrined in an elegant temple in the Theban Hills just beyond the west bank of the Nile near Luxor. Nefertiti's likeness appears on more of the world's souvenir shelves than Napoleon's. Cleopatra inspired millions of dollars worth of movies and perfumes and as a result will forever be mistaken for Elizabeth Taylor.

But a woman who may matter more for the Egypt of the here and now is a relatively obscure entrepreneur of 45, the mother of three children. She is an Arab and a Muslim, the cultural duality in the Middle East that is historic but not known for opening corporate or political doors for women.

Samya Abd Aelazeem makes women's clothing in Cairo and sells to factories in competitive bidding. A few years ago, she did some calculations. She needed a loan, relatively small by corporate standards but not by the standards of small business in the poor countries of the world. The sight of ordinary people with meager resources walking up to a loan officer's desk seeking money for a struggling business is no more enchanting to the operators of commercial banks in Egypt than it is in the Philippines or Peru, or for that matter, the United States of America. So Samya Abd Aelazeem went to an organization called CEOSS on the recommendation of a friend.

CEOSS is a Christian-based developmental and lending institution in Egypt, the Coptic Evangelical Organization for Social Services. Samya worships in a mosque.

Business cooperation bringing together Muslims and Christians in the Middle East is hardly new. But in the climate of post September 11 it has more than casual significance. Yet the most notable side to Samya's adventure into business was her risk as a Muslim woman in an Arab country, staking out terrain in a part of the world where women have for centuries been consigned to silence, scrubbing, and child-bearing. In some of that world, they have lived for generation after generation in a veiled non-personhood. That has begun to crumble, but only begun. The suppression is not so severe in Egypt, but you don't see a Samya every day. And when you talk to her, you are moved by her spunk and her energy. You are also moved by her utter belief that she is making a difference, not only for her family, but in some indefinable way, in the lives of women around her.

She is a woman of brown hair, brisk movements, shrewd eyes, and spurts of quick laughter. A white scarf covers her head to the edge of her hairline, but this is a woman who is not going to be bulldozed by tradition or sexism. She is also not going to be much fazed by religious rigidity or by the generally accepted limits of 24 hours in a day.

She came to the Coptic service for a loan to boost her cash flow for a business she had operated for a number of years. Long before that, she had discarded the clock and the calendar as any meaningful regulator of her time. Her parents died when she was five. When she was old enough to work, she became the principal support for seven brothers and sisters. She married an engineer and developed a hobby making dresses and discovered she could do it well. She also had an eye for design. Why not, she asked herself, put this to work?

So she bought two sewing machines for $500 on credit, and in 1987 began selling dresses to small factories. The buyers liked the dresses. She bought more material and eventually found a workplace of her own where she could produce in larger volume. She was beginning to acquire a reputation for skill and reliability. But she kept sifting through the ads in the Cairo trade papers. Factories were inviting bids on uniforms for institutional and company use. The orders seemed substantial to Samya. They did not seem over her head. Ideas began singing in her head. She had a design for this company and the right cut of uniform for that hospital. But she didn't have the cash to buy material in lots big enough to put her in the competition.

She drew out her plan for the loan officer at CEOSS. She could bid on those contracts if she had 3000 in Egyptian pounds, something under $1,000 in American money. CEOSS examined her operation and the loan officer looked at her intently to take a measure of this woman. What he saw was confidence and energy. He also saw an unmistakable eagerness to hit the bricks and asphalt in pursuit of a goal. CEOSS gave her the loan at the normal 14 percent interest, a few points under the commercial rate.

Samya's imprints were on the market within days. The cash fluidity she now acquired put her in a position to buy more material and to land those more lucrative contracts. They opened the way for her to expand the services of the factory she'd created for herself. It wasn't much later that she was pledged another loan. The factory manager, Ahmed Frat, was frankly astonished by the woman's drive and her minimal requirements for sleep. Note that Ahmed Frat is male. The factory owner, Samya, is female. She is, therefore, Ahmed's boss. Egypt is an Arab, Islamic country. That fact didn't seem to influence Frat's genuine admiration for Samya or his obvious enjoyment in working for her

"She sometimes goes home at 3 o'clock in the morning," he said. "She's back in a few hours. She is amazing. I call her the 'iron lady.'" Her competitors may not be so kind. Practically all Middle Easterners are congenital marketers, and the competition, while occasionally good-natured, tends to develop bared teeth. But it is an environment in which she flourishes. She has been careful not to be devoured by obsession that would cloud the true focus of her life. Her oldest daughter is a law student at Cairo University. A younger daughter is also studying there, probably headed for banking. The family's youngest, a boy, wants to be a pilot. All of these goals seem to be within reach, buoyed by their mother's determination to give them every chance.

Without the boost from microcredit, it would be a goal more distant. The iron lady's ultimate goal is to maximize the quality of life for her children. She wants them to know that. So from time to time she brings material home from the factory and works with it at home to teach her children how it becomes a dress or uniform. This is a corporate woman who still feels a powerful need to fill her role of motherhood. So if something has to give, it's the clock. She turns its face to the wall. Samya is in the factory, or in the house, or in the market, all in the same day.

Does this define some kind of modern Egyptian wonderwoman? It probably does. Not everyone can or wants to blaze those trails. But without seeking public applause from women who hear her story, she recognizes that women in Arab countries, Islamic countries, need models. She steers away from any blatant political rhetoric. But she says, "I want more and more women to have opportunities. We're not all alike. Some women have to stay home and raise the children. But I know many women here who are capable of a stronger role in their communities that would give them more satisfying lives."

An American visiting in Cairo asked her if she's bothered when she sees television pictures of women under suppression in Islamic lands.

The woman clearly disavows a political life. But she is, nonetheless, a woman of her time.

"When I see that," she said, "I'm . . ." She paused. "Annoyed," she concluded. In private, she probably would have made that stronger.

But without much question, she is part of a mounting wave of women's involvement in the business life of parts of the Middle East, a movement nourished by the new opportunities afforded by microcredit in addition to some glimmers of modernization. Without the will to modernize, it's clear the Arab-Islamic nations are certain to be imbedded in a ever deeper economic poverty that might further destabilize the politics of the Middle East and world. Because of this, the empowerment of women like Samya Abd Aelazeem becomes an important nutrient toward the modernization of a part of the world that just five centuries ago boasted the most advance civilization on earth. Now, most of the Arab Middle East is imbedded in a cultural straitjacket of one form or another: an autocracy ruled by dogmatic religious mullahs or billionaire sheiks or paranoid military strongmen. The visitor to Egypt is struck by the juxtaposition of forces. There is the power of an entrenched religion whose dogmas, like those of any other religion, can be murderously perverted. There is the incredible architecture of Egypt's antiquity, the enormous wasteland of the desert, and the struggles of modernists to make headway. There is the drift of a government wanting to speak for the Middle East but lacking the moral authority and the charismatic leader to do it. And through all of this threads the lifeblood of Egyptian civilization, the river Nile.

The river Nile is the most important, indestructible fact of life in Egypt. It is the wellspring of whatever economy exists and the source of its history and its glory, vanished now but graven for the eons in its marvels of stone and art. It bears witness to collision of three great religions and to the grief of the poor and hungry for whom the river, for all its strength, cannot provide enough nurture. From a hotel balcony the visitor can look down on the Nile, flowing somehow immortally. There are very few sights on earth that can bring you face to face with the sweep of the ages as evocatively as the Nile. It immerses you in the beauty and power of a world that was, and yet simultaneously lifts you disturbingly into the chaos of the Middle East that is.

For Egypt, one of the curses and the amazements of the world of the here and now is the urban monstrosity of Cairo, now approaching 18 million in population. It sprawls for miles across the flanks of the Nile Delta to the edge of the pyramids. If the pyramids and the Temple of Karnak and the tombs of the Pharaohs are the dead soul of an Egypt gone forever, Cairo is its penance. There are people who have scraped up a thousand dollars to buy dwelling space in one its ancient graveyards. Slums abound. Penniless people flock to Cairo from the villages along the Nile where they can't make a living growing or selling sugar cane. There are practically no services in some of those places. But there are in Cairo, as hapless as some of them are. And yet the visitor finds Cairo irresistible. There's that quality in the Museum of Antiquities, where all of those old dead Pharaohs are lovingly perpetuated in their arsenals of coffins, headdress, and interminable false beards. Cairo seizes the imagination of the visitor who grew up on a film diet of North African intrigue and double-dealing in the shadowy atmospherics and slow-turning fans of dens and smoky cafes. But there is also elegance in the floodlit minarets, and of course, the Nile by moonlight.

Can the principles of microcredit work here?

"Of course," said Wafaa W. Khalil, a woman who heads the development services of CEOSS. "They are working. They can't solve the problems of poverty in Egypt by themselves. But they are a way. The struggle we have is to increase funding. We need to bring in more clients and to make the system pull its own weight, make it sustainable so that it doesn't depend on grants. Our organization (not the only one involved in microcredit in Egypt) has 2 million clients who get the benefit of service and training and care in things like education and health, but only 2,000 clients of microcredit."

Why the slim roster?

Almost all of its money now comes from American nongovernmental agencies like Opportunity International and from sources in the United Kingdom and Germany. The American government's USAID once was a contributor, but not now. The Egyptian government is notoriously strapped. Funding from Egyptian sources for social service and startup capital was more available years ago under a socialistic regime than it is now that a market economy has taken over. The country's main revenue producer, tourism—for which it can thank all of those moldering pharaohs and their tombs—has taken staggering hits in the last four years from terror incidents, war, threats of war and a sluggish world economy.

But what about the Egyptian tycoons often seen at the casinos of the world and at its most luxurious spas?

"When businesses in Egypt give money for humanitarian purposes," Wafaa said, "they like to put the company's name on it. So they often give to big projects they can be identified with."

This is another uncommonly strong woman in a male-run society. She is 47, multilingual, single, and self-sufficient. The daughter of a Presbyterian minister in Egypt, she has pursued an education from Cairo to Canada to Harvard in economics and management. She identifies herself as Christian, Arabic, Egyptian, and African. That is a mouthful and a handful, and sometimes it has to put her on a tightrope. Although she has been in the social service business too long not to be emotionally affected by the needs and unfairness of the distribution of wealth in the Middle East, she is also a hardskulled business administrator. If you took a loan from her organization, you're going to have to repay it in the time allowed, or it's the last one. The repayment rates for her clients are nearly 98 percent. But because many of the loans go to businesses already running, and because this is Egypt, only 35 percent of the borrowers are women—which compares with much higher percentages in microcredit around the world.

Wafaa said:

"We can't give to every small vendor. We try to reach some of those with group lending, where the small borrowers get together and guarantee each other's loans. We want to bring more women in. But most women have all they can do to bring up their children. You have to understand that. Still, more women are moving into non-governmental work like this in Egypt, and more are moving into senior management.

That is important."

Does she feel tied down by the historic barriers to the advancement of women in the Middle East?

"I'm a woman. As a woman I have all the rights I need. I'm using my education. God has created us to do something with our lives, to have goals and to achieve goals. When I've worked in the fields or anywhere that was available to me, I opened a window to look at the whole world. I don't think it's religious tradition that is holding down women so much in the Middle East. Some people may be using the name of religion to give their causes credibility. But intrinsically, it's not the religion itself that would be suppressing women. It's the political traditions that suppress them. It's not a lot of fun being a woman with ambition if the political system closes the doors. Sometimes the political and religious cultures do that together. So what are we looking for as women here? Women want the right to express themselves. And what happens when they do? In our programs, we find the women are more committed than men. Their goals are higher, perhaps because they haven't had the chance before.

"What I see among the women in our programs is the need to make every second count and to live more, to be committed to a life that is something better than what they've had. In Iran, for example. Iranian women are seeing what women are allowed to do in the rest of the world. I saw a wonderful Iranian woman at a conference in Holland. She was leading the discussion on rights and self-expression, what is possible when women have a chance to behave as powerful personalities.

"What I know is that those things are coming to more women in the world, and they are already here for some of us."

A man listening to her at the small gathering we attended in Cairo was Bahaa Kamel, a parttime government employee who had made side money for years selling flypaper in Cairo.

That's correct. Flypaper.

Consider the intrinsic worth of a humble ribbon of flypaper. The product is indisputably popular here. It's going to acquire that approval in any place where flies historically flourish. Eventually, competitors overcrowded Bahaa's market in Cairo. He looked for another venue and found it making candles. For a couple of years he made candles by hand. It was laborious, but satisfactory. It also was barely profitable. But he saved enough from his government job to buy a candle-making machine, which he installed in his apartment. When Bahaa married, he and his wife moved into a new apartment and converted his old one into a workplace. His wife became a co-worker. In the morning Bahaa worked for the government while his wife made candles. In the afternoon he joined her. Their specialty was brightly colored candles.

"Egyptians love color," he explained.

And why is that?

There is one very prominent color in Egypt. Marketers in America call that color "sand." They don't have to call it sand in Egypt. It's more or less understood. When you subtract the 6 to 12-mile strip in the valley of the Nile, what you have in the rest of Egypt is the Sahara. It's somewhat monochromatic. So Bahaa and his wife made blue candles, fire engine red candles, pumpkin orange candles, and more. Among his several admirable traits, Bahaa is a promoter. He went to the military, which maintains gift shops. He went to hotels and tourist centers, peddling candles of all lengths in a multiplicity of designs. The hotels and resorts liked his inventory, and he needed money to expand. The commercial banks weren't interested, but Wafaa Khalil was. She approved a first loan of $1,250 and a second of $2,000. Bahaa produced new lines of candles—candles in the form of black cats with wicks between the ears, candles depicting the pharaohs, pyramids, and the old temples. Sales jumped. He hired an employe. And eventually he found another market: Christian monasteries in Egypt, of all places. From Italy he found reproductions of The Last Supper and spread them with a layer of perfumed wax, comparable, he said, to the fragrances of the ointment that the women daubed into the linens in which Jesus Christ was wrapped after the crucifixion.

This in Egypt of the twenty-first century.

You can call that a little different, but it's also microcredit. Bahaa recalled the words of Samya, the clothing designer.

"With the right chance," he said, "we can all make it."

The ones more likely to make it are the ones with the good sense to avoid selling flypaper in Egypt.

CHAPTER 13

An Answer to Thieving Bureaucrats

W hen poor folks gather with their cash to make their loan payments in the bush, money piles up in stacks on the crude tables. Most of it is crinkled and faded. The treasurer counts it once, twice, three times, and then asks a partner to count it again.

That is about as sophisticated as the bookkeeping gets. It's highly conscientious. But it's primitive. There are no platoons of battle-dress security police patrolling the grounds. There are no hidden cameras or magic eyes, either. But this is the money of people trying to fight their way out of nowhere. For that reason, when the microcredit managers in their distant offices thousands of miles away in New York or Washington hire administrators to run their operations, they aren't going to pick candidates with dreamy eyes and vows to save the world by next Leap Year. If you're going to manage microcredit money, it's acceptable to have a tender heart. But what you need more realistically is a hard head.

Microcredit is often a last resort for people in countries where an extra two dollars a day can be the difference between life and death for children in the house. If you're monitoring the cash flow from an umbrella agency in the United States and you want to see a successful operation under those conditions, you face some crucial truths of economics that can't be dodged. Sloppy accounting, naïve leadership, and fuzzy planning will bury a microcredit organization, with destructive consequences to potentially thousands of people. This is what's at stake: Well-meaning people donated that money as an investment in and for the ambitious poor. When those grants and donations get to the counting tables of the small and vulnerable borrowing groups around the world, they materialize as cash. And if any of it starts disappearing under the table or into strange pockets en route to the village bank, the people you want running the show in New York or Washington or Nairobi of Kathmandu shouldn't be inspired mediocrities who discover the larceny six months later.

What you need are managers with a banker's brains for the numbers, with marketing savvy and the unsentimental eyes of a Matt Dillon when those numbers look fishy.

Harold Jastram, a lawyer and board member of one of the most respected microcredit foundations in the world, FINCA (Foundation for International Community Assistance) lays out FINCA's mindset on how to operate in a way that protects both the investors and the borrowers. Its rules and charter are as clear as the whack of a judge's gavel.

"We don't let people steal from us or from our donors," he said. "We have affiliates in 20 countries. The first thing you have to know is that sort of thing is a rarity. We find a remarkable level of honesty in the handling of money right down to the counting of it at those village banking tables. But when we find that the numbers coming out of one of those places don't add up, we go after the suspects. And we do it aggressively."

How aggressively?

In one of the Central America countries a few years ago, FINCA discovered that some women had stolen money belonging to a village banking group. The organization put a bounty on every lamppost it could find and launched a search. It also alerted law enforcement agencies. "It cost us $30,000 to find the thieves," a FINCA manager said. "But we did. They ended up in jail. We found the ringleader covering her career as a thief by working as a room maid in Las Vegas. She ended up in jail, too. What we wanted to do was to give a message to our clients and the people who handle money all over the world: If you steal from little people and helpless people, we're coming after you and we're going to find you."

The microcredit institutions that uniformly deliver the strongest performances are the ones with FINCA's kind of creed of top-to-bottom diligence. In some ways, it is the polar opposite of the mentality that crept into the highest echelons of America's mega-corporations in the late 1990s. The modus operandi among some of the biggest money-crunchers was to exploit the stock option culture to amass vast personal fortunes. It was done with shell-game accounting tricks that were either demonstrably illegal or palmed off as slipshod accounting by the political apologists for the multi-millionaire sandbaggers. The losers, of course, were the shareholders, gullible employees who invested in company stock, and the public—which ultimately will pay the price.

Compare that with a hard line gospel on ethics set down by Jastram's FINCA organization. It was founded in the 1980s by John Hatch, one of the creative leaders in microcredit and a pioneer in today's version of the village banking method. Hatch came out of the Peace Corps and an earlier career of developing new rural programs in the poor countries. In the middle of that he worked on his doctoral thesis as a hired farm laborer in Peru. With that kind of experience, you're going to know something about what works in Third World economics. The FINCA organization he built searches restlessly for innovation in the field to stay with—or ahead—of the times and cultures. One way it does that is to listen seriously to the people it wants to help. All of that gave FINCA a clear-headed focus on where it's going.

Here is Jastram on clear-headed focus:

"We keep rigorous control of our system. Yes, there is this Third World culture of stealing and bribery. Not everybody does that by a long shot, but we're going to be sure it doesn't move in on our operation. If one of our managers in the field is losing control of his accounts and losing control of the paperwork, we fire him. We're not political and we're not partisan and we're not tied in with a particular religious faith. The integrity of our operation is crucial to us. It means our clients, the poorest of the poor, have somebody looking after their interest and we're not going to bend the rules. They see that and they trust us. You don't often find our clients—poor people who are trying—getting attacked when there's guerrilla warfare in those countries. I asked John Hatch about that and he looked at me and said, 'Harold, it's simple. Guerrillas have mothers, and most of the people who are receiving those small loans are mothers.'

"We're not trying to set any kind of political agenda, but I really believe that education and teaching people how to work and manage money in their own economic system is one way to settle the world down. The people we work with now have jobs and are earning their way in the world, where they can see something better and have hope, and people like that aren't going to crash airplanes into skyscrapers or kill their own people. Microcredit is one way to make the world safer. The people who work through it can still be considered poor in many ways, but they are no longer humiliated people who have to beg for money. The fact that they pay back those loans—and in our organization it's something over 97 percent—tells you something about integrity."

FINCA took a traditional system of communal banking, one practiced in many cultures as a means by which the individual borrower or saver could count on the group as a backup, and modernized it with disciplined accounting methods and trained management. It called its own model of communal savings and borrowing Village Banking, and spread it to anybody who wanted to borrow it. In the process of establishing tight controls of its systems, FINCA avoided some of the self-serving errors that characterized part of American aid in the past.

"John Hatch crystallized the idea that much of the United States aid in the past had been misdirected," his brother, Bob, said. Like Jastram, Bob Hatch is a member of the FINCA board in Washington. "It went something like this: Congress would ask, 'What can we do to help this American farm machinery manufacturer? What can we do to get some export sales? Let's send these tractors to the folks in Peru.' The problem with that is that the folks who can buy farm implements in Peru aren't the ones who need help. The ones who need help are the ones who are making a dollar a day, or less."

And why are they so incredibly conscientious about repaying those loans? Bob Hatch said:

"They are at a place in their lives where this loan—which we call small by our standards, $75 or so, is a last resort. If they're going to break out of generations of poverty, this is their last best chance. The reason that the great majority of the borrowers are women is that women are the moms. In most of the poor countries, it's the moms who get stuck with the kids. The father is no longer around, for whatever reason—illness, working somewhere, alcoholic, off to war, killed in war, whatever. The mom is often the only parent raising multiple children. There's no safety net. There's no assistance from the government. What happens if somebody gets sick? So the mother is forced to turn to some kind of enterprise to feed and care for the kids. If she goes to a money lender on the street, she's going to be taken advantage of. The loan sharks will manipulate her payments to 95 percent of what she could possibly make. She'd never get ahead."

The Village Bank is a fundamental, no-frills method of bringing money and savings plans to people who can't afford them in any other way. The virtue of village banking is that it allows its members a voice in who gets the loans, how the repayments are collected, how the savings are managed and how the group solidarity can become a powerful resource in training and education. An even more critical benefit is the role of the village banking group as collateral for the borrower.

What this system does is to take the basic principles of commercial banking and put them on a level where the clients, the overwhelming majority of them being women, can work their small enterprises using the same banking practices as corporate giants. It means, for example, that these women will come to each meeting with their homemade ledgers to record their transactions and will have to sign notes for their loans in the same way millionaires do at the Wells Fargo.

"I'll never forget the admiration I felt one year when I spent time in Honduras," Bob Hatch said. "Women were signing notes for their loans. Fully 80 percent of those women signed by stamping the note with their thumbprints. They couldn't write."

The scene is chiseled in Hatch's memory.

But—

"Five years later in Honduras I witnessed a similar scene. And 80 percent of the women signed their own names. While they were taking their loans through the years, building their small businesses, they were also going to school."

And the respect he felt went deeper.

What are those businesses? You'll see them in the big open-air markets in South America, Africa, Indonesia, India, and in a thousand venues. The small entrepreneurs will be operating fruit stands, selling rice and beans, selling shish kabobs, fixing bicycles, running tiny, closet-size kiosks that look like convenience stores because they *are* convenience stores. Or they will go door to door selling flour or sugar or clothes or thread and fresh fish. Whatever sells, whatever's needed. They may not have to deal with the fine print regulations of peddlers in more industrialized countries. But these are poor people who want a better life for their kids, and beyond that, most of their customers know the peddler from a long way back. A lot of this business is neighborhood fare. And it is what FINCA and scores of organizations like it were organized for—giving people a chance, opening the door for them to do something with their lives beyond scavenging for the day's meal for their family. For the poor as well as for the prosperous suburbanite in America, there is a point where a dream intersects opportunity. Poor people *do* dream. The flashpoint comes when they run with the opportunity.

"But one of the fascinating parts of offering people the chance to take small loans like this," Bob Hatch said, "is the discoveries you make about different cultures, and how those cultures affect the direction that this vehicle, microcredit, takes.

"The huge percentage of microcredit borrowers around the world obviously are women. But when you operate in Albania or Kosovo in the Balkans, for example, where the Muslim religion is strong, the figures go upside down. Those places are still male-dominated societies. They are among the few places in microcredit where the male borrowers outnumber the women. And yet our one model basically works anywhere, and it's amazing what you discover about the cultures that you're trying to accommodate. In the Village Bank model, the typical number in the group in South America, for example, is 30. That makes sense. If you have half that number, it costs twice as much in overhead to serve that group as it would the larger one. But when we put in the model in Russia, we found we couldn't find more than eight or nine people who were willing to form a group."

Was some form of anti-social behavior at work here?

"Well, no, not exactly that. The phenomenon we found was that most of the clients were suspicious about working with larger numbers, because that would bring in people who were strangers to them. And these people, maybe eight or nine women familiar with each other, were suspicious about the others if the group got larger. We found that attitude traced to the authoritarian society in which they'd lived practically all of their lives. What they were worried about was informers in the group."

It was a wariness bred by decades of mistrust. It meant that in this particular culture, the village bank groups tended to be extended family instead of the broad spectrum of the community that defined the village banks in South America and elsewhere.

"But we also found in Russia that the people who entered these small entrepreneurial banking groups were remarkably well educated, and their repayment rates were right up there close to 100 percent. There was one woman in particular, very attractive, about 32 years old. She asked a question about the gross margin of fashion goods sold in America. I said 50 percent might be a gross margin. She looked at me and seemed quizzical. She said, 'Is that calculation on sale price or cost?' I'm not kidding. I used to run specialty retail for a big company and I had store managers who couldn't answer that question.

"This woman began taking loans of $65 to $85 in Russian currency over a four-month period. She said she wanted it to buy material for a fashion store in Samara in eastern Russia. Her family once ran a metallurgy factory in that town, or rather she did. Times went bad. The factory closed. Now she was going into the clothes business. She couldn't do it in an outdoor market. It gets pretty snappy in winter in that town. Colder than Minnesota. She had these rinkydink stalls to work with in an old basketball arena, an armory that served as a market center. The stalls were chain-link boxes 15 feet high and 10 or 12 feet deep. That was her space. She put hangers up there to display the clothes, and she knew her business. The stuff sold. She went through five loan cycles with us. When I visited she showed her workplace, and then she said, 'Now, let me introduce you to my employees.' She'd done so well that she was hiring.

"She brought the employees over. Each of them is running a little shop. Now she has three stores in that complex and probably will have more."

It started with a $65 loan. When people tell you Russians don't know about capitalism and market economies, take a train and check out the dresses in Samara.

FINCA's operational control might be tighter than some in microcredit. Its direction comes from its board in Washington and the specialists who work for the organization. It maintains hubs in the areas in which it works, such as South and Central America, Africa, Eastern Europe and in states of the former Soviet Union. It is careful about the on-the-ground managers it hires in the developing countries, but the ultimate expertise, auditing, and therefore control resides in its board. But the beneficiaries are some of the world's poorest.

FINCA gets money from U.S. government assistance agencies, world development groups, foundations, and individuals, enough to buttress more than $135 million in loans around the world in 2002. It makes a continued effort to lift its operations to that desideratum of microcredit, which is "sustainability." That is the level where a village bank or a microcredit institution has enough money in hand to give it the leveraged capital to manage its loans, savings and interest without new donations. But, Bob Hatch acknowledges, "no matter how efficiently we manage the business, we can't grow without donations. This means planning our cash flow carefully. Everybody who donates wants to give to the loan program—which means they like seeing their money going directly into the hands of the borrowers who wants to build a little business."

In other words, Foundation X or Donor Y wants assurance that their money is going to the woman in Zambia who needs a sewing machine to make clothes to sell.

But some of that money has to be directed into operations to guarantee the reliable auditing that is at the heart of successful lending in the developing word. Some of it has to go into quality control. Some of has to pay the accountants and marketers who make the system work. That is not as dramatic as the gratified smile of the woman in Zambia.

"But you have to have it," Hatch said. "Still," he said, "in 2002 we spent 82 percent of our incoming money directly on our loan programs. We spent another 16 percent on operations and just 2 percent on fund raising."

Those are audited figures. They constitute a remarkable performance, good enough to permit FINCA to operate in Haiti, under economically wretched and politically tense conditions. And it was attractive enough to begin operations in the former Soviet state of Kyrgyzstan, where it recorded the fastest growth in demand for services in the organization's history. In just five years the program in Krgyszstan reached 18,000 clients, plus self-sufficiency.

Success like that was impressive enough to permit FINCA to join another major microcredit provider, ACCION, in being listed among America's Best Charities (or services) by Worth Magazine.

Not coincidentally, another organization that prides itself on innovations to reach the poorest, Freedom from Hunger, headquartered in Davis, California, made that same list. Freedom from Hunger is 50 years old. It was in the field a lot earlier than most of the microcredit providers of today, and it somehow has kept ahead in new ideas by putting flexibility ahead of formulas. "Give mothers the resources they need most, and they'll do the rest," says Freedom from Hunger's Chris Dunford, one of the respected innovators in the humanitarian aid industry.

Freedom from Hunger insists on tying education to credit. It often works with commercial credit unions in the 15 poor countries where it operates. And it's relentless on the point of providing education and training (in family planning, disease prevention, basic nutrition, breast-feeding, prevention of HIV-AIDS, and business management) in addition to its microcredit loans.

The delivery systems in the remote reaches of developing countries aren't going to be sophisticated. Here is Freedom from Hunger's Tom McBurney, a former food executive with the Pillsbury company, describing them:

> "We train local people and the local credit groups eventually become autonomous. We want it that way. We have trained agents in a number of villages who get on their motor scooters and introduce the program to other villages. That guy on the scooter is important to us. He brings the village banking groups together and he dispenses some of that practical education that saves babies' lives. Those small borrowers in the village banking circle are disciplined in how the bank. They keep minutes, and they repay their loans on time. We sometimes work with partner groups, which is one way to give the life-saving education the women need; and those trained loan officers are another. So adding the education component to credit is not expensive."

Does that work? Freedom from Hunger has 200,000 loans out this year. It has made loans totaling over $98 million to women living on less than $2 a day, and nearly every cent has been repaid.

The foundations and governmental agencies that provide seed money to FINCA and Freedom from Hunger readily endorse numbers like that. Yet an even more powerful endorsement may be the one from Dominga Perez, a 50-year-old weaver in Nicaragua. Although she and her husband, a laborer, both worked, they weren't making enough to feed their children. A FINCA field worker visited her community and suggested that Dominga should organize a village banking group. She was reluctant. In fact, she was afraid. Borrowing money might put her family at risk of losing what little they had, or put them further behind. She juggled the idea in her mind for a few days and decided to go for it. "Our lives would never change if we didn't take a chance," she said.

She formed "Weavers of the Lake" with 48 other women. The rules were that money had to be repaid weekly as part of a four-month loan cycle. Of the money they borrowed, 20 percent had to be set aside in savings, leaving 80 percent of the loans to put into a business. The rules also provided that the next loan would be based on the accumulated savings, meaning the more a member saves, the more she can borrow. Research showed that as those little businesses grow, family income doubles or triples, and so do the food purchases the family makes. This in turn means that as those loans are obtained and paid off, then recycled, the family's health and nutrition improve immediately. The projections show that once launched, that business will produce nine loan cycles over three years and an average savings for the borrower of $300—the equivalent of thousands of dollars by American standards.

"With God's help," Dominga said, "I think I will buy sheets of tin roofing to add a second room to our house. It's time my patojos (children) have a place of their own to sleep."

This woman took more than a risk. She took her family to a place where it couldn't have imagined two years ago. And she will tell you today it wasn't that much of a risk. It was "good business," she will say, sounding a little like Bill Gates.

But you and I know it still took guts.

CHAPTER 14

Small Entrepreneurs Flourish
Beneath Himalayan Giants

K athmandu, Nepal—

Travel posters that invite tourists and trekkers to Nepal depict a country irresistible to the adventurer. The Himalayas are stupendous. They reveal a startling white world, the highest and mightiest on earth. Yet not many miles to the south, Nepal's Chitwan jungle is a dominion of elephant and tiger.

The picture is not oversold. Among the faraway places on earth, Nepal appeals almost instantly and magnetically to the explorer and seeker.

But its poverty and tragedy reveal another Nepal that on the surface is one of the horrors of humanity. In Nepal millions of people live below subsistence levels; orphaned children by the thousands live on garbage piles or are enslaved; young women are forced into prostitution, transported to India and elsewhere. The misery seems endless. In the spring of 2001 the country's future king went berserk in the royal palace and massacred his family before killing himself. Within a few months of that slaughter, the seven-year-old Maoist insurgency had forced a suspension of parliamentary government, sowing political chaos in a country that could barely stay afloat even in orderly times, with so little to export.

But if you can take the time (and accept the risk) of traveling today in the remotest parts of one of the poorest and most politically inept countries in the world, you make some remarkable discoveries. One of them is the thousands of women who are liberating themselves and their families from the manacles of poverty and oblivion.

Microcredit works in the most improbable places on earth. You see that in Uganda and in the mountain country of South America and in the debris of civil war or political oppression or even threatened famine in the Far East. But Nepal is a little harder to imagine.

In some places in western Nepal, loan officers administering village banking groups sometimes have to walk days to reach a weekly or monthly meeting. In the hill country of western Nepal not long ago, members of a self-help banking group were meeting in a sparsely-furnished village hall when armed Maoists walked in and demanded to know what the meeting was all about.

The program officer stood at the bookkeeping table with a handful of small rupee notes and tried to explain what was happening. These women were meeting, he said, to vote on appeals for loans by members of the group. They needed to bring more money into their little businesses and their families. The Maoists wanted to know what kind of money they were talking about.

"One or two thousand rupees," he said. It translated into $13 to $25 if you converted rupees to American money. Nobody was converting anybody's money in the presence of gun-wielding Maoists on that day, or doing much except looking at the barrels of those semi-automatic weapons.

One of the Maoists demanded a month's pay from the edgy program officer, who stood too terrified to speak.

"How much money do you make?" the Maoist leader asked him.

He gave the figure and emptied his pockets.

The Maoist scowled and then grumbled. "I'm making more than you are," he said. "Go on with your meeting." The patrol walked out of the building and disappeared.

The staying power of the microcredit idea and the commitment of its members and its sustaining staffs around the world sometimes surprise hardboiled money handlers and humanitarian experts alike. Maybe it shouldn't be that surprising. The human spirit lifted by hope and spurred by incentive or desperation is not easily defeated. Although Americans are long conditioned to the power of the enterprising spirit, they often overlook it when they're confronted with the poverty of less advanced parts of the world.

Can the poor be driven, and their lives bettered, by the same help-yourself, get-ahead mentalities that we revere and romanticize as "American" qualities?

Of course they can. You're not going to see the mothers-of-six, deprived of property, turning themselves into millionaires in Nepal. But you will find women there by the thousands who have discovered qualities within them that they wouldn't have imagined a few years ago.

And why not? A country like Nepal is not gifted with charismatic populist leaders. Its rural areas are remote from basic services and sometimes from the most rudimentary communication. But in the last 10 or 15 years the communal banking and savings concept has managed to create footholds in the semi-literate countryside, encouraged by the introduction of a still-primitive political democracy in the country in the late 1980s and by the assistance of western agencies and donor groups.

The most vulnerable of the poor in Nepal, as in most of the developing world, are women. Their plight is especially aggravated in Nepal because of societal and inheritance traditions that keep land in the hands of men. Women can work their way out of the system or through the system, but it sometimes takes extraordinary persistence, iron will, and the small miracles of microcredit.

To find out how that's come about, later in these pages you'll meet a fascinating woman from New Zealand named Helen Sherpa, who more than 20 years ago met and later married a bright and ambitious young exchange scholar from the Solu Khumbu mountain country of Nepal. While he became a respected forestry and conservation expert in Nepal and Tibet, she entered the microcredit industry in Kathmandu and now is an overseer of programs that have elevated the lives of women throughout Nepal. But to get your first exposure to women on the rise in Nepal, you have to thread your way through the noisy minefields of traffic in the streets of Kathmandu, where most of the microcredit of Nepal is administered.

Kathmandu is the Nepalese capital, the site of its royal palace and major temples and the brokerage center of the country's limping economic system. It is the home of thousands of peddlers and shop-keepers who serve both locals and the tourists drawn by the great mountains and the exotic appeals of Kathmandu itself. Here is a city that gives you the essence of The East with all of its squalor and mystique. The air you breathe in urban Kathmandu sometimes reaches choke levels with its dust and pollution. Its streets are impossible to keep clean and orderly; children and young mothers and invalids beg openly. But there is something here about the antiquity of the Exotic East, about the babble of the streets, about the struggle to find a way, that many who come to Kathmandu find captivating.

From a city hotel—The Shangri La, what else?—to the office of Mukunda Bahadur Bista, it's a taxi drive of 15 minutes through the chaotic streets. There's a certain no-guts-no-glory code about driving the streets of Kathmandu. It governs all traffic, taxis, private cars, motorbikes, rickshaws, and overloaded buses. The faint-hearted have two choices: They can walk or go back to the hotel, but they do have to get out of the way. There *are* traffic laws and rules, but almost all of them yield to pure gall, which is the bedrock clue to survival if you want to risk driving in the streets of Kathmandu. Our driver was endowed with all of the necessary self-preservation techniques and got us to Mukunda Bista without damage or actual trauma.

Mukunda Bista is executive director of a non-governmental organization called the Center for Self-help Development (CSD), begun a little more than 10 years ago in Nepal to reduce poverty. Among its current affiliations is one with Women's World Banking headquartered in New York. Mukunda's office is on the second floor of a tidy but nondescript business building not far from one of the main commercial sections of Kathmandu. The walls of its conference room are hung with flow charts and the updated mathematics of the microcredit movement—current membership numbers and projected expansion. It is a rather proud effort to define the advance of microcredit and its possibilities in this struggling country. Mukunda Bista is slightly-built, courteous, and accommodating. His English comes across lyrically—and sometimes hypnotically to the visitor—in that wonderful lilt that identifies the speaker as a native of India, Pakistan, Bangladesh, or their neighbors of the subcontinent. He knows those numbers are impersonal but critical. They record the reach of his organization's work in the bare decade that it has tried to bring financial services to thousands of people in Nepal on the verge of oblivion.

But he also knows that each one of those figures represents the face of hope and a higher horizon for thousands of families. CSD got help in the early going from governmental and private organizations in the Netherlands, Japan, the United States, and other countries in addition to the central bank of Nepal. Its principle arm in providing small loans, almost exclusively to women, is a Self-help Banking Program (SBP) that was founded with the infusion of seed capital from the Grameen Trust of Bangladesh. But today the self-help banking movement in Nepal gets no direct support from the Nepalese central bank apart from a soft loan. But it has been able to meet its operational costs through income from the interest it draws in lending to thousands of poor women. That is a remarkable performance in a country as shaky economically and politically as Nepal. And those thousands of women, incidentally, aren't as poor as they were before they took the first step in what's now called the Grameen model of group lending.

Let's say you're a woman living in the Udayapur district of Nepal. This is not hypothetical. The woman is Kushmi Devi Bisokarma, now in her early 40s. She married early, which almost all Nepalese women do. Her husband was a blacksmith who owned no land but was making it marginally in his trade. Eventually they had seven children, a family too big to be supported by the blacksmith's slim wages. Kushmi helped with some skills she learned from her husband. However, if the family has seven children, the woman isn't going to be doing much at the forge and anvil. There wasn't enough food to feed nine mouths. Kushmi started making trips to her mother-in-law to borrow some grain. In the extended family, Kushmi's pilgrimages to her mother-in-law became a joke. Humiliated, she had to stop borrowing from the relatives and start taking loans from the local loan shark. The interest was 5 percent a month, and it was endless.

In time she had to start working for the loan shark without pay whenever he asked her because she kept falling further behind in her payments. Somewhere about then her husband got tired of the struggle, mostly hers, and walked off to find a job that paid more in another town. He decided to stay there. That left Kushmi in the lurch with six children to feed and clothe in their sagging old hut of a home (one of the children had died in a fire).

Kushmi had long ago discovered that panic is not an option for a Nepalese mother of six. She asked herself what she knew that could bring in some money. What she knew was basic blacksmithing. It's an occupation not high on the list of potentially lucrative work for women in Nepal or any place else. But Kushmi started looking around for capital to launch her on her new life. Without credit from somebody, she was going nowhere. In the midst of her explorations, she heard about an SBP loan program in her village. She asked around and learned about village women planning to form what SBP calls a "pre-group." This is the traditional Grameen group of five that undergoes training in how apply for loans, how to save, how to deal with interest, and what microcredit can mean in salvaging lives. The Grameen group of five eventually is folded into a "center," or a community of 40 made up of eight sub-groups of five. Kushmi joined four other women who qualified for the center, became a member, and applied for and received a first loan of 2,000 rupees, or approximately $25.

With that money, she began investing in equipment. Through the group and through educational sessions with agencies linked with her savings and credit center, she learned something about marketing: what to make that sells and what kinds of markets to sell it in. She hit on a couple formulas. Farm equipment is always in demand in rural Nepal. If you make it sturdy enough and price it moderately enough, you're going to sell. What else was there? Well, almost all women, in Nepal or New Jersey, love gold ornaments. She couldn't very well sell in New Jersey. But she knew her way around the Nepalese bazaars.

Kushmi had months in which to pay off her loan, and she did. That transaction qualified her for another loan, this time of 5,000 rupees, and then another of 10,000 rupees, more than a hundred dollars if you converted to American money.

Before long, Kushmi Devi Biswokarma was practically an all-star lady blacksmith, bringing in enough money to underwrite wedding ceremonies for four of her children.

Today she is making more than $10 a day in her trade, a stratospheric number by Nepalese standards. She recently bought some land in the market district where she built a new house. At latest count, her assets approached a thousand dollars. And today the neighbors no longer smile and snicker when Kushmi Devi Biswokarma walks by.

"Without the loans," she said, "none of it would have ever happened."

Without the loans, yes. But the impetus for them came from Kushmi, her determination to find a life for herself and her children.

All right, why are these small loan programs invariably described as "almost exclusively for women?" The phrase virtually defines the worldwide microcredit phenomenon. It is the linchpin in bringing working capital to the poor in every poverty-racked country on earth that has been opened up to microcredit.

Mukunda Bista was asked why it works this way specifically in Nepal. He said:

> "Yes, the loans are made to the women. This doesn't mean
> that all of the women who receive loans in Nepal use them to
> build their own small businesses. Often there is a partnership
> involving husband and wife. I'll give you one case among the

more than 37,000 borrowers we've reached in our savings and credit self-help groups and centers. A woman wanted her husband to get started on his ambition to become a barber. She took out a small loan as a member of one of the women's group. With that loan she bought a pair of scissors that launched her husband into the hair-cutting business. With a pair of scissors! You don't see many barber chairs in Nepal. He started going to marketplaces with that pair of scissors and began attracting customers. He did it aggressively. 'Hey, your hair's too long. I can make you look terrific.' Soon those scissors were bringing more income into the family and the woman took another loan. But this one was to make steamed rice wrapped in vegetable leaves to sell at the market, so they were both running little businesses.

"What this program does is to give great numbers of women an economic power they've never had. Most of them are tied to the home most of the time. So they've never had a chance to earn money independently. Now they're learning that small loans can put them in a business if they budget their time to build that business in the hours they can spare. People ask, 'why not lend to men?' Women happen to be the more responsible borrowers. Why? Women find it easier to fit into groups. They build networks more quickly and build trust among each other more quickly. Men are more competitive. Women also tend to be more practical and reliable borrowers because, you have to remember, they've never had this opportunity before—having access to money, being able to save, making choices about what to do with money. And finally, women are still the caretakers of their household. When you lend to a woman in Nepal, you know that whatever money she makes from that loan for a business it creates or expands for her, that money is going into the household. We hear that in some cultures men resent women taking on this role. But we don't see much of that in Nepal. In most cases the man understands that the benefit goes his way, too. There's more money coming into the house, and often it boosts him up in his own work."

It may not be a shock, therefore, to learn that the repayment rate on those loans to more than 30,000 women in Nepal's SBP programs was 100 percent at one of the most recent counts and has been staying there for years. And yet for all of the impact of those figures on the uplift of women in Nepal, a single scene in a meeting hall sometimes overpowers the statistics. Here is a woman, for the first time in her life writing her own name instead of making her mark with a thumbprint. It's what she learned in the group meeting the day before. She looks at those little loops and whirls at the bottom of the page. Together they form her name, one she has never seen before. And she has written it. Her identity, who she is, is suddenly more vivid and more precious to her. It is a gift she had never foreseen. She can write her name. She weeps. And so do the women at her side.

That has become possible because literacy programs are now increasingly linked with the small loan programs in Nepal. Changing the lives of women in Nepal, it was obvious from the beginning, had to start with literacy. This is a country where 78 percent of the women cannot read.

It is where we meet Helen Sherpa, once of New Zealand, now part of the literacy and microcredit breakthroughs in Nepal. She and her future husband met while both were students at Lincoln College of Canterbury University on the South Island of New Zealand, where Helen grew up. He was one of the academic stars among the Sherpas of Nepal. He had received a scholarship under the auspices of one of the programs organized in Nepal by New Zealand's Ed Hillary, the conqueror of Mt. Everest and now a virtual saint in the eyes of the Nepalese for his lifelong humanitarianism in their country. Helen's husband became a leader in the conservation and cultural restoration programs in Nepal. She assisted for a time, mothered four children, willingly planted potatoes and gathered cow dung for fuel with the other Sherpa women and finally decided to make more productive use of the energies and commitments she brought to Nepal.

Helen Sherpa is a strong and engaging woman. She is verbal and inventive. Her mind is a corn-popper full of a dozen ideas a day for building better lives for the poor of Nepal. Some of those ideas eventually brought her in contact with organizations such as the Women's Economic Empowerment and Literacy (WEEL) of World Education and the women's empowerment program of PACT Nepal. Major development organizations such as the USAID, the World Bank, and the Ford Foundation have been players in those programs, also World Neighbors along with agencies from France, the Netherlands and other western countries. Most of these link literacy and health education with credit and savings programs of some kind. Combined, those programs and others like them have reached over 100,000 women in Nepal.

This is the rather stunning report from PACT:

" In just one and a half years, 90 percent (of PACT's) female clients have passed a literacy test and (through microcredit) have saved the equivalent of over $1.2 million during this period. The astonishing success of (PACT's women's empowerment) not only proves that the poor embrace learning but also that the poor have the desire and capacity to save."

It's not done with mantras and mirrors, Helen Sherpa of World Education's WEEL will affirm:

"There's no question these women are motivated. But what you have to know at the beginning is that they have been denied opportunities and property, and they sometimes have no clue about how to get going with a business, how make use of these small loans to build more income for the family. Most of that is rooted in their lack of education—knowing basic math, literacy, all of that. So that's where we begin.

""You can simplify the language to make it easier, but there's not much you can do to change the mathematics of borrowing and saving and buying and selling and marketing. So we look for creative ways to present the math, and we're looking for more. Already we're finding that using fake money in teaching math helps these women. We try games to make it easier for newly-literate women to understand the math, remembering that a lot of these women live in remote hill villages where they don't have many opportunities to use it in their daily lives.

"Women of Nepal are making it. It makes one humble just seeing that. But first they have to grapple with some basic truths. Most of them just don't understand the disciplines required in becoming borrowers, paying loans, and saving. They don't understand the risks involved in committing to a loan. They need to plan, which they haven't done before."

Helen Sherpa, the World Foundation supervisors discovered, was a natural as a tutor. She'd lived as a Nepalese woman, understood their lack of savvy in dealing with money and marketing and their limited literacy. She also understood their toughness to make it if given an opportunity.

"But here's an idea of what they had to get past: Women of the Terai, the southern jungle of Nepal, make great baskets. So when microcredit was offered there, basket-making was an obvious scheme. So they should make baskets for sale at the Christmas season, somebody said. That sounded great until somebody else said, 'Wait a minute. They're not going to make those baskets on time. They make baskets only in the winter after the Christmas season, when the grass is dry. They're not going to drop everything they're doing and start making baskets in the off-season.' So this super marketing plan went poof. That was the trouble with a lot of the thinking when it came time to launch small loans for women. You had to adapt those loans to the reality of people's lives.

"There's a classic story about women getting together to put all their potatoes in a big pile in one of the bazaars of Nepal. What they found was that the biggest and the best potatoes all went first. At the end of the day they were left with the smallest and least saleable of the potatoes—because all of them carried the same price tag.

"At the next women's group meeting somebody said, "Hey, how about putting different prices on the big potatoes, the medium potatoes and the small potatoes?"

They did. At the next potato sale the cost-conscious consumers eventually bought all of the potatoes. Helen Sherpa explained:

"What happened in Nepal was that when micocredit scored its first big success in Bangladesh using the Grameen model, government here began jumping on the bandwagon. It created loan projects with seed money. While the intention was good, the process was all wrong. You can't impose an idea like microcredit and communal banking and saving—which requires both trust in the group and self-reliance in repaying the loan—from the top down. It has to go the other way. The way it was first set up, the borrowers could see the seed money as the donors' money or the government's money. They acquired that loan money, shared it out, and disappeared. When you reverse the process and take out a loan from what is in fact the group's money accumulated by savings, you're dealing in "hot money," in other words, your own money. The other, donor or government money, is "cold money." That's what they call it.

"So the idea became: Most of this is "hot money." You can pour in a little bit of "cold money," or donor money, to keep the thing lubricated, but if you put in too much cold money, the formula is wrecked and the magic is gone.

"In other words," Helen Sherpa said, "the borrowers essentially have to own what they're doing. The very first requisite of village banking is that the group has to have confidence, trust, in itself. It makes decisions and votes loans for the individual members. The trust goes two ways. If you don't have that, you don't have anything."

Outsiders are often amazed that the repayment rate on these loans to the poor, semi-literate or illiterate people hovers constantly around 95 to 98 percent.

The answer, of course, is trust. The poor woman will take a risk when she believes that her friends will stand by her if she falters. And they do stand by her. If that's not present, the laws of the economic jungle take over.

Is it any wonder that the number of savings groups in this impoverished country has climbed past 20,000, and you can multiply that by the 40 or so people who are members of each of these groups? And what does that say for "development" in a so-called undeveloped country? It means this: there is enough new income being produced by those poor people to bring into the house a gas-operated cooker called a gorba. They can do this with the loans for which they're eligible after proving their reliability. People who now burn firewood never get enough firewood, and the collection of it can tear up the environment. Those cookers burn cow dung and other combustible wastes. The result is a gas for cooking and sludges that make good fertilizer. The cookers cost around $300. Some of the borrowing groups are now voting loans to their members for the purchase of these cookers. One member gets a loan this time around, another the next time.

To the rest of the world, this may not look like hotshot development. But if you've been poor and you live in Nepal, Helen Sherpa said, "it's development, all right."

"The reason this is a pretty electrifying thing in Nepal is that historically, women just haven't been able to do this. All of the economic privileges were conferred on men. If women wanted to get something on credit, they had to go through their husbands who could put up collateral with the bank.

The savings and credit groups have worked a kind of liberation. And it means the big thing for women now is borrowing
for their children's education. It's not only love involved here.
They see it also as an investment. They don't have many safety
nets in Nepal. If the children are educated and able to find
productive work, they can better care for the parents in their
old age. And that leads into medical care. Historically, Nepalese
women have never put themselves first. They might have
needed medical care, but they didn't ask for it because they
couldn't spare the money that might be needed for the children. But now, women can actually borrow money for primary
medical care."

That transformation of thousands of women from household
drudges to at least part-time entrepreneurs has been extraordinary to
people who know the barriers facing them. Most of this new market
skill has come through the workings of microcredit and the gentle
prodding of unsung program officers like Laxmi Ghimri, who works
with Helen Sherpa and is some kind of Nepalese father confessor and
confidante of the women with whom they work. "He's a wonder
because he listens," Helen said. "They've got all kinds of problems that
they bring to Laxmi, and he calms them down and shows them a
better way, but they love him because he listens, which is the way to
the heart of almost any woman."

So staff work is critical, and it can sometimes produce startling
results. "Microcredit alone isn't the answer," Helen Sherpa said. "It has
to be combined with agricultural development, literacy, health care
development, and a half dozen other tools. We advocate with the
government for these people. We tell our people you have to priori-
tize when you go a government center. You can't give the guy in
charge a laundry list of needs. You might get that new road you need
without asking. But if you really need training in how to grow ginger
or health care for goats, and that's number one for you, all of you
better go down to that district office together and lean on those
people with one voice. Thirty women clamoring for healthy goats can
be intimidating to a district officer."

That it can. And a little prodding with expertise can change the
lives of a lot of women. In the Bardia jungle area of southwestern
Nepal lives one of the poorest ethnic groups in the country. An
epidemic of malaria brought villagers out of the hill country and into
the lands of these jungle people and pretty much dispossessed them.

Helen's jungle women's credit group needed help. "Laxmi came in with an idea. These people were fixated on cutting and sewing as a project. Craft work. Laxmi said, think again. If 30 women are going to do crafts, you're all going to compete with each other and nobody makes money. They had 80,000 rupees to work with. So they did a feasibility study."

A what?

"A feasibility study. It's something women of Nepal have learned about. The result of their deliberations was to invest the rupees in garlic. They rented a piece of land from a wealthy landowner and grew garlic. It was a terrific investment. Another group not far away passed on garlic and said, we'll do potatoes. They did and made money. A third group grew winter wheat. Nobody cut one piece of fabric for craft sale. And every group made money."

Is that development?

"It's the human spirit," Helen said, "when it's given a chance."

CHAPTER 15

20,000 Women
20,000 Mobile Phone Booths

Whenever journalists and historians put together a roll call of heroes in the struggle for social justice, India's Mahatma Gandhi is almost invariably the first to be enshrined.

His political goal was to free India from colonialism. But the surmounting cause of his lifetime was to liberate the powerless from hunger and humiliation and to goad those who live in comfort and safety to extend their arms, as neighbors, to those who live in hell on earth.

Gandhi was murdered before the microcredit movement began to lift millions of those people to a place he would have applauded and with a means he would have endorsed.

He said this:

"Whenever you are in doubt . . . apply the first test. Recall the face of the poorest and the weakest man whom you have seen, and ask yourself if the step you contemplate is going to be of any use to him. Will he gain anything from it? Will it restore him to a control over his own life and destiny? True development puts first those that society puts last."

History's most powerful movements of liberation are those that confront an injustice so offensive that it ultimately must fall before the mobilized forces of conscience and common sense. The final sentence in Gandhi's testament speaks with the same unflinching call to humanity as the witness of Martin Luther King Jr., Nelson Mandela, and others who have led in the struggle to relieve the afflicted. It is a timeless assertion of what is right. And what is very right by the standards of Mahatma Gandhi is the mission of microcredit when it functions best. Because of the huge numbers of poor people it has already freed from the worst of poverty, microcredit's still-evolving mission puts it in the ranks of some of the most powerful movements of social revolution.

The idea is that human beings deserve to be free. They should have the freedom to harvest every grain of their potential, if they have the will and energy to do it. Most of the liberation movements have needed martyrs to ignite the passion and mobilize the voices and the will power of the oppressed. Transforming ideas, revolutions, often do.

But now here is the palpable injustice of global poverty. It has been built into generation after generation, ingrained poverty recycled in the undeveloped lands of the earth and made a condition of life for hundreds of millions of people.

It does those people little good now to demonize the colonial powers who finally got out to save their hides or gave way to somebody's higher conscience. What the poor need today is not the guilt of their former custodians, but their credit in the bank. The beauty of the microcredit movement—and it is big enough and now has legs enough to be called a revolution—is that it doesn't need martyrs. Nobody takes prisoners or operates first aid stations at the weekly meeting of 50 women clutching their bankbooks and their loan payments in a churchyard strewn with banana fronds in Arusha, Tanzania.

That's the one significant difference that sets apart the microcredit movement—giving poor people access to capital—from the other social transformations. Slavery disappeared in most of the civilized world after wars were fought to end it. The sprawling old empires that exploited millions of the illiterate and helpless have slowly crumbled in the face of violent rebellion or the rich countries' own territorial wars in Europe.

But microcredit doesn't have any enemies worth identifying. When it works right, which is most of the time, everybody is better off—the small borrowers, the lenders, the big corporate benefactors in America and Europe, and even some of the autocrats in power in the poor countries. Nobody's head is in danger.

The revolution fostered by microcredit recurs every day around the world and begins almost wordlessly. People we call nobodies take somebody's hand. In that hand is a small loan. With it they buy some corn or a beat-up sewing machine or some pots and pans. With those they start building a business. And then the hands they depend on are their own. They pay off the first loan and take another loan. They start saving. They are now enterprisers. For them, the world changes. They can now sing and dance.

That is how a new life begins for millions of people today.

Is poverty so ugly an injustice that overcoming it can suddenly make people human?

The one man in the world with indisputable authority to talk about confronting world poverty is Muhammad Yunus, the founder of the Grameen Bank. Not coincidentally, in New York in the fall of 2002 he received a humanitarian award named in honor of Gandhi. Yunus has never deviated from his message, and his words stick. They don't shift to accommodate the audience. The power of his vision and his commitment have breathed life into the once-dull and beaten eyes of millions of people who had been abandoned as hostages to the ruthless culture of poverty and oblivion. His idea is simple and un-yielding. Its premise begins with a condemnation.

"Human beings," he has said a thousand times, "were not put on this earth to live like animals.

"When they have to spend the night looking for scraps of food to prolong their lives or feed their children, they are animals.

"When they have no shelter against the night or against the storm, they are animals.

"Human beings need to do more than to survive. They need to have joy and hope in their lives, and more than a billion people in the world today have neither. They have a right to that as human beings."

Momentarily, he stands mute at the speakers' lectern. The over-head lights seem to streak his eyes with indignation. That is something of an illusion. Here he is not an angry crusader. He is calmly indict-ing the waves of civilization, over the centuries, for their callousness and their inhumanity.

And then he says quietly to his audience of bankers, credit under-writers and money brokers: "I think you know now that poor people have dreams like all of us do. They can be trusted, like you can be trusted. Give them access to a little money to start. They might amaze you."

And, of course, they often do.

Yunus pours out energy and mission, but his mercurial personality needs room to express the full catalogue of his moods. He's an entertainer as well as a lecturer. At a podium he swings easily into the character of an academic imp. He grew up in the education system of Bangladesh, got comfortable with the American idiom and economic hot buttons as a scholar in this country, and then launched his microcredit schemes on his return to Bangladesh.

His colleagues at conferences around the world wear the western suit and tie. Yunus is a man of the East, and yet a man of all continents. In public daily he wears his olive vest and a tidy beige workshirt, buttoned at the color. They are his work clothes and his uniform. He didn't invent microcredit. But in packaging microcredit to the simplest denominator—a group of five women, acting together, borrowing together—he eventually popularized it on a global scale. But first he had to sell it:

"Well, the first thing the big banks in Bangladesh did was tell me I was crazy. I told them poor people can be good risks and they showed me the door. I told this guy, I said, would you be convinced if I told you we tried this in five villages, and it worked?

"He said he wouldn't be convinced.

"I came back and said we tried this in 10 villages and it worked in every one. Does that convince you?

"He said it didn't convince him.

"This guy couldn't accept that poor people can manage their money as well as rich people, or even manage it better. But the idea spread quickly through Bangladesh, and it was working in hundreds of villages and then thousands. And then I went back to the big central bank and the guy said he was convinced. And so I told him it wasn't right that great masses of people didn't have adequate housing in Bangladesh but they would if we could give them a $100 loan to start a house or to improve the one they had. I drew up a plan and he said it wouldn't work. I asked why not? He said my loan plan didn't meet the definition of a house.

"So I tried it another way. I said the house would actually be a small factory. I said, 'Look, this family needs a place where it can make pots and jars. It needs a place with a roof on it so their little business wouldn't get washed out in the monsoons.'

"He said, 'No way; that doesn't meet the definition of a house, either.'

"I tried another way. I told myself maybe this idea of a house is a little too grand, so I called it a shelter instead of a house, and he rejected that idea, too.

"Finally, I came back and said, "Look, these people have proved they repay their loans. They pay their bills and they're good citizens and they're reliable, but they need a place to work and to live and to eat and sleep and they need a house where they can do these things and build their lives. And so I gave him that plan and he said, "Okay, we'll do it.'

Muhammad Yunus tried, but not very hard, to restrain a giggle. "Now I'll tell you something. Years later we got the great, prestigious Aga Khan International Architectural Award, and we've made a half million housing loans and there's been a perfect rate of return recovering those loans."

So what are you, Muhammad Yunus, some kind of archangel of microcredit around the word, a patriarch?

The professor waved his arm dismissively and offered a better ID. "I'm a streetfighter," he said. He meant advancing house by house, village by village, pushing microcredit joyfully and obstinately, stepping on the lumbering toes of Institutionalized Banking and Historic Stereotypes of the Poor. And over the years, those villagers swelled into the multitudes because Yunus' message, and the message of both his disciples and the hardheaded money leveragers that he won over, was the same: Decomplicate the process. Let the bankers and investment wizards and idealists argue over whether the whole shebang ought to be sustainable or whether social development goals ought to come before bringing in more money to poor households.

One will inevitably or almost always follow the other, Yunus said. He carried that message with his free-winging arsenal of persuasion that clearly included—but was not limited to—a quick and rational mind, charm, a light hearted pugnacity and a refusal to be deflected by those glares of disbelief among the financial goliaths.

It is the forces of history, and the simmering violence of the twenty-first century, that often goad Yunus into a more intense attitude of evangelism when he talks about humanity's critical stake in bringing hundreds of millions of the world's poor to the thresholds of opportunity. These opportunities are now reserved, he argues, by the industrial powers.

A delegate to the Microcredit Summit international conference in New York City in November of 2002 asked him how critical that was in bringing some lasting stability to the world politically and socially.

"I don't know if there is anything more critical."

The idea, the delegate began, is that reducing the number of the poor reduces the threat of destabilizing . . .

Yunus flared. His own hot button is the easy temptation to confuse the poor—people who live in poverty—with the conditions of poverty and how they were created.

"It's *not* the poor. Yes, by reducing poverty in the world you can lessen the threat of more World Trade Center atrocities. But if we try to solve that problem by military means, we're on a terribly wrong track.

"It's not the poor that created the conditions of poverty. Poverty is created by policies, by social injustice, by attitudes, by greed, by traditions of power. Look, there are always going to be Bin Ladens. There are always going to be radicals, extremists, and vengeful people. Today people worry about radical Islamics. Not long ago, people in America worried about the Ku Klux Klan. There have been unreasoning, violent voices for thousands of years, but now they are even more dangerous. What we need to do is change the way we look at people who are outside (the industrial mainstreams of the world). We need to realize it's not being poor (that alienates many of them), but the sense of rejection, that nobody is paying attention to them.

"It's this feeling of rejection that can build up support for the radical voices. So we need to show concern for neglected peoples so that the Bin Ladens will not find supporters. If you deal with their problems, as microcredit has been doing, you empower millions of people by bringing new values into their lives. When you do that, this is what happens: These people can say, 'Now I've got something. I don't have to listen to those guys.' So frustration can come with poverty, but poverty comes from political and social and economic injustice. Once you lift people from the bottom, you're doing something about that injustice.

Reconciling the races and cultures of humanity, appealing to the best that is in them and warning about pandering to the worst, is as much the heart of Yunus commitment as his social evangelism. He's not coy about confronting Americans with the abuses of their own injustice and with drawing a picture of what might have been even more horrendous consequences if they didn't react to those abuses.

"If one ethnic group is always at the bottom and another is always at the top, you have the conditions for conflict and hatred. If this country (America) hadn't changed the way it treated black people a hundred years ago, the way they were still being treated in the 1950s, I think you might have seen what terrorism is.

"But now you see that you can have a white person and a black person working in the same office and they don't think about being white and black the way they used to. You can have a black person who is the Secretary of State. That is what it means when you help to lift a people out of poverty. You see that it can be done. You see that those people didn't create the poverty, but they were pushed into it and kept there for a long time. And so what we're saying is, give poor people around the world a chance to use their ambitions and their energy, and you will change the world forever."

Eventually Yunus modified his basic model of small groups—small loans, recycled over and over—and moved into the new terrain of optional individual loans and creative formulas for repaying those loans. Some of his current repayment theology is generous: "As long as they're paying something on that loan, they're not defaulting." The Grameen system he fostered in the Far East is still at core a group lending plan to build the tiny enterprises of millions of borrowers. But it is moving microcredit into loans for pensions, insurance and other social safety nets.

Not all of Yunus' schemes are noisily endorsed by his associates and competitors in the microcredit field. Some of these people are frankly tired of his visibility. But when he speaks about the power of microcredit to kindle the human spirit, to save lives, to give an identity to a child orphaned by AIDS, the distance between Yunus and his listeners evaporates. Their intimacy is electric. He has instantly created a community. His message is simple, uncluttered, and vibrant. Poor people can be trusted. They can overcome. They will be back tomorrow and the day after that with their tiny payments because now they have something to live for.

Charisma, though, will take microcredit only so far. It has proved its value, but to go dramatically further it must be taken seriously by the world governments with the resources. The United Nations sets aside some funding money, but the United Nations is a meeting hall of the governments of the world. And governments tend to give money to governments when they start funding relief programs, which often is an invitation to the disappearance of money into the hands of slippery-fingered bureaucrats and functionaries. It's corruption, and it has hijacked billions of dollars that could have kept masses of people alive and put millions of kids in schools.

Microcredit, on the other hand, is administered privately. So the anxious glares and appeals of the aid seekers usually wind up with a direct vector on Washington, D.C. There, of course, are the biggest resources in the world—plus a half-century of serious global involvement in humanitarian or, broadly, foreign aid. Those investments have shrunk miserably over the years, and in the opinion of many of the internationally minded in America, unforgivably. They have done so partly because of the increased cost of today's high tech military equipment, the development of which has made America the unchallengeable world Colossus. But America's world outreach has also been the victim of partisan politics as well as the diminished interest of the American public—fed by the spectacle of cycles of corruption by thieves in government in the lands of the poor.

Yunus knows all that. But the times, he is saying—both the threats and opportunities of today—are too important to wring our hands over the relatively small cost of befriending the world's poor with money they can use to improve their lives.

In today's volatile world, how do you compare that with the risks of not doing it?

He appeals for serious thinking in America about the power and potential of microcredit as an important force in the reduction of poverty around the world and in the good will America inevitably would harvest from it. While the microcredit movement has acquired wider interest in Congress, it is hardly a serious rival in the hearts and heads of most elected politicians or administration budget writers to, say, American farm subsidies. Sam Daley-Harris in Washington is the Microcredit Summit Campaign director and a man with a bulldog disposition in guarding the interests of the poorest of the world's poor. He is incensed that the United Nations—while devoting some resources to microcredit—insists on relegating microcredit to the rank of "a footnote" in its catalogue of the established tools for lifting millions out of the slag piles of humanity.

That is where millions do live today.

And it is where microcredit performed its most powerful transformations in the some 30 years it has been a lighthouse for a better life for voiceless people adrift in poverty.

Are they really that? Transformations? If you doubt it, consider this: the addition of $2 or $3 a day in the pocket of the average American citizen may not be much. It may, in fact, be the difference between a cup of decaf regular and of a double caramel latte at this afternoon. All right, you can throw in a small muffin.

But in a barrio in Mexico City, that extra $2 a day can buy the medicine that may save the life of an ailing child.

The extra $2 came into the house because the mother got two loans of $50 each to buy the material to make clothing for the market.

Multiply this family by 50 million. That is transformation. The $2 a day that can buy you a more sophisticated cup of coffee can be the equivalent of $25 dollars a day or more for somebody who needs to save a life or educated a child.

That figure of 50 million families is not hypothetical. It is where the advocates of microcredit expect to be approaching the year 2004 in bringing small loans to the world's poorest families. They hope to reach 100 million within a couple of years after that. And if so, they would be approaching a halfway point in an ultimate goal of reaching the estimated 1.2 billion people now living below the poverty level. That figure, of course, has to be divided by four or five, which would give you the approximate number of families living in the lowest poverty.

And how do those figures translate, 100 million families, meaning 500 million people, with access to money for the first time in their lives? In the calculations of the Microcredit Summit Campaign it would mean life-saving better health and nutrition for tens of million of families; tens of millions of children would be able to attend school; tens of millions of families would live in better homes; tens of millions of families would have a higher status in the family and community.

And what would the benefits be to our world and our lives in the simple humanity of uplifting all of those poor, in the reduction of hatreds and alienation caused by hunger and illiteracy and powerlessness?

The benefits to all of us are beyond calculation.

But are these numbers a fanciful exercise in the what-could-be?

Until he gives you a reason to discount his wisdom, you'll want to give Muhammad Yunus a respectful ear.

"We can reach that 100 million," he said. Economic booms and slides, he says, come and go. The simplicity and the *effectiveness* of microcredit sticks. "It isn't all smooth like high financial people would like it to be. It takes time for this to pay its way." Institutions that could do more to build it, he says—big foundations, governments, and investment banking—would like better and faster returns. "All those things are true. But we *have* to build it."

How?

More of the prestigious banks are looking at it seriously. They are doing so both for investment and as an avenue—through loans guaranteeing the performance of microcredit banks—that can appeal to their clients' dual interest in (a) humanitarianism and (b) at least a slim profit for the record and their entrepreneurial pride. Big corporate and family foundations represent a significant bloc in the indexes of microcredit donors and sponsors. These include such international stars in the corporate, investment and foundation firmament as Calvert, Deutsche Bank, Citigroup, Monsanto and Charles Stewart Mott Foundation. There are dozens of others. But it's probably true that any major new infusion will have to come from the Congress of the United States. The movement has already acquired first magnitude political allies. Vincente Fox, the Mexican head of government, is one of its most passionate advocates and has pushed through some important enabling systems to expand microcredit in Mexico. Fox makes the critical distinction between government that can lubricate microcredit and government that can strangle it by attaching political strings to its endorsements.

In the United States, there has until now been a refreshing bipartisan support for the microcredit idea among elected politicians in a position to bring new resources to it. The support of Senator Hillary Rodham Clinton may be prophetic. In New York in November of 2002, she made the point that "poor people have collateral beyond their blood, sweat, tears, and hard work. So part of the of the unfinished vision of microfinance is to alter the minds of the powerful about the powerless. (It is also) to provide a vision and an international platform for respecting what poor people bring to the table." The governmental and non-governmental agencies can institutionalize that respect, she said. They can do it "by beginning to provide property rights and by recognizing that access to credit is often denied not because it is expensive to provide, but because it is a tool of oppression used (by the powerful in their countries) to keep people poor instead of opening doors to greater opportunity for them."

So microcredit's mission, she said, and especially the mission of leaders and industrialists who understand microcredit's strength, "is to transform hearts, minds, and attitudes . . . changing the attitude between the powerful and the powerless around the world."

It's possible that a single, resounding statement or call to action by the most powerful figure in the world, sitting in the Oval Office in Washington, could almost instantly impel that change in attitude. The day may not be all that far off. It is something, at least, to be hoped for.

In view of its pressing urgency to expand, microcredit's achievement in little more than 30 years has been astonishing. If it does reach its goal and raise from poverty somewhere close to 100 million of the poorest families, it will have come from almost nothing in the 1960s and '70s to somewhere more than 30 million of the poorest families today. It means microcredit advocates, its corporate angels, and its clients have tapped into a vein of human longing and human vigor that may eventually in the twenty-first century transform hundreds of millions of the once-ostracized poor into a new global middle class.

Is there some social and economic revolution in America with which that outcome can be compared? There's at least one. The trade and labor union movement in America, scorned and almost dismembered by the industrial heavyweights in the early 1900s, gained strength and respectability in the Great Depression of the 1930s and in World War II. Within decades, its members, once scraping by on scarcely a living wage, had by the late 1940s and '50s graduated into the swelling ranks of America's middle class, delivering fresh earning power and vitality to the American economy.

And many of their children today are upper middle class suburbanites and rather proud to call themselves conservatives.

The burdens of the poor in the world's undeveloped countries are infinitely greater than they were for the American poor. But one of the absorbing parts of expanding microcredit is the ingenuity it has attracted both among its clients and its brainstorming advocates. Those idea people roam the world, dabbling and experimenting, and often, as in the case of Jonathan Campaigne's franchise system with Pride Africa and Scott's Hillstrom's pharmacy shops in Kenya, they will unite microcredit with local investment. Small itinerant grant makers fill the holes that microcredit can't because it costs big money to reach the rural poor. Slowly microcredit is being brought into insurance, health, education, and home-buying programs for the poor. High-level risktakers like Bill Drayton and his ASHOKA offer an entirely different kind of inducement to local entrepreneurs—three-year grants to change the way their local society works, how it delivers education, how it breaks down the drug traffic, how it motivates kids, how it builds communities.

The time when microcredit was regarded as the penny arcade of social and economic empowerment of the poor has long gone. Today hundreds of millions of people are involved in it around the world. They have been brought in initially with some form of western money, whether offered to local microcredit institutions for pure humanitarian reasons or in some enlightened self-interest that ties poverty reduction to more bank deposits or American security. It doesn't matter. Those two mainstreams eventually flow together as the nourishment of giving. Compassion in itself, in the words of the Dalai Lama, is the single most divine of human attributes.

But ingenuity doesn't hurt.

Muhammad Yunus in his irrepressible early days as the Pied Piper, the Poet, and the People's Banker of microcredit showed the way. In his cat-and-canary stories of how it was done he portrays the establishment bankers as the skeptical heavies, but it does it with a wink, because he and microcredit need those people. He's going to break you up with the great cell phone coup. Cell phones started to come into the 1990s in Bangladesh. Nobody had the money there to make wire phone calls, and hardly anybody had the money to buy a cell phone.

"Microcredit can put a cell phone in the hands of everybody in Bangladesh," Yunus announced to the big bankers.

"Impossible."

"The way it can happen," he said, "is one woman in a village takes out a loan to invest in a cell phone. She offers the use of the cell phone to the rest of the villagers and gets a small transaction fee for that, which eventually pays for the cell phone. The cost to the user is very small. Everybody in the village will use it."

"Let's see it happen," he was told. "Most of the women who could buy the cell phone can't read."

"It doesn't matter," Yunus said. "The keypad of the cell phone isn't very complicated. All she has to do is to learn 10 numbers."

They tried it out. In a matter of weeks the first woman in the village who bought the cell phone had memorized the area codes and the city codes of every major country and metropolis in the world. In a short time, everybody in the village was using the single cell phone.

The idea caught on in the next village.

"Eventually thousands of villages in Bangladesh bought into the system," Yunus tells us, "and today what do you have?"

We are prepared to be amazed.

"You have 20,000 women in Bangladesh functioning as mobile telephone booths."

If those women ever graduate to automobiles, General Motors, Ford, Toyota, Mercedes, and Ferrari will all move to Bangladesh.

A Microcredit Contact List
For Potential Donors and Supporters

For further information on microfinance institutions, their programs, and how to contribute, we offer the following list of selected resources and websites. There a hundreds of fine microcredit programs, microfinance institutions and related groups, but we chose the more prominent ones, as well as:

- those groups mentioned in the book narrative,
- a few humanitarian organizations that, realizing the power and effectiveness of microfinance, have added it to their core services,
- organizations that are also network and training institutions (indicated by an asterisk★), and
- important sources of information

IMPORTANT SOURCES OF INFORMATION

★Microcredit Summit Campaign: www.microcreditsummit.org

Information: The Campaign is the largest repository of information on microcredit institutions and networks, their programs, status, geographical locations and current issues.

Statement: The Microcredit Summit Campaign is "working to ensure that 100 million of the world's poorest families, especially the women of those families, are receiving credit for self-employment and other business and financial services by 2005."

Publications: *The Microcredit Summit Campaign 2002 Practitioner Directory; Pathways Out of Poverty: Innovations in Micofinance for the Poorest Families.*

Microbanking Bulletin: www.microbanking-mbb.org/bulletin.html (past issues available on line)

Microfinance Gateway: http://nt1.ids.ac.uk/cgap/index.htm (a project of CGAP and ELDIS)

Consultative Group to Assist the Poorest (CGAP): www.cgap.org

PBS series on microcredit and microenterprise development: "To Our Credit" www.pbs.org/toourcredit/home.htm

Prominent Microfinance Operating Institutions that Raise Funds for Microloans

* ACCION International: www.accion.org
* ASHOKA: Innovators for the Public (social entrepreneurs, some involved in microfinance): www.ashoka.org
* BRAC (Bangladesh): www.BRAC.net
  Bank Rakyat Indonesia (BRAC): www.bri.co.id
* Calmeadow (Canada) (training): www.calmeadow.com
* Cashpor (Malaysia): www.cashpor.com
  Credito con Educacion Rural (CRECER) Bolivia: www.crecer.org.bo
* Finca: www.villagebanking.org
* Freedom From Hunger: www.freefromhunger.org
  Global Partnerships: www.globalpartnerships.org
  Grameen Bank (Bangladesh): www.grameen.org
  Grameen Foundation USA (information and fundraising unit): www.gfusa.org
* Grameen Trust: www.grameen/com/grameen.gtrust
* Katalysis Partnership: www.katalysis.org
* Opportunity International: www.opportunity.org
* Pact: www.pactworld.org/Global/Microfinance/html
  PlaNet Finance: www.planetfinance.org

- ★ Pro Mujer: www.promujer.org
- ★ PRIDE Africa: www.prideafrica.org
  Self-Employed Women's Association (SEWA) Bank (India): www.sewa.org
- ★ Small Enterprise Education and Promotion Network (SEEP): www.seepnetwork.org
  Sustainable Healthcare Enterprise Foundation (pharmacies financed through microcredit): www.shefoundation.org
- ★ Trickle Up (pre-microcredit grants): www.trickleup.org
  Village Enterprise Fund (pre-microcredit grants): www.villageef.org
- ★ Women's World Banking: www.womensworldbanking.org or www.swwb.org
- ★ Women's EDGE (advocacy for women in aid and trade negotiations): www.womensedge.org

As an addition to these and other microcredit institutions available to potential donors, the authors of this book have established a fund to receive contributions from individuals who wish to help the ambitious poor. It is the Miracles of Microcredit Fund, which will be maintained by The Minneapolis Foundation, one of the country's major community foundations. Because it is a certified non-profit entity, contributions to Miracles of Microcredit are tax-deductible, as they are to the other fund-raising institutions listed here. If you wish, you can designate your preference for a country or part of the world to which you would like your contribution sent. Contributions should be sent with your name and address to Miracles of Microcredit, C/O the Minneapolis Foundation, 800 IDS Center, 80 South 8th St., Minneapolis, MN 55402. The authors' websites are www.jimklobuchar.com. www.adventuresingiving.com.

Humanitarian Organizations with Microfinance Programs

- ★ American Refugee Committee (ARC), which works with refugees in transition and enlists microcredit to develop income for them: wwwarchq.org
- ★ CARE International USA: www.care.org
- ★ Catholic Relief Services: www.catholicrelief.org/what/over-seas/enterprise.cfm

* CEOSS (Egypt) www.ceoss.org
* Heifer Project International: www.heifer.org
* Oxfam: www.oxfam.org
* Save the Children Federation: www.savethechildren.org
* World Education: www.worlded.org
* World Vision: www.worldvision.org

For Information on Investing in Microfinance Institutions

Calvert Group: www.calvertgroup.com

Deutsche Bank: www.db.com/community/micro/index.html

Citigroup: www.citigroup.com/citigroup/corporate/fndtion/
index.htm

Some Multilateral and Government Organizations that Fund and Advise Microcredit Programs

African Development Bank: www.afdb.org

Asian Development Bank: www.adb.org

Canadian International Development Agency: www.acdi-
cida.gc.ca/microcredit

Inter-American Development Bank: www.iadb.org/sds/MIC/
index_mic_e.htm

International Fund for Agricultural Development(IFAD):
www.ifad.org

Sustainable Banking for the Poor (World Bank):
www.esd.worldbank.org/html/esd/agr/sbp/

U.S. Agency for International Development (USAID)
Microenterprise Innovation Project: www.mip.org

United Nations Development Programme (UNDP) – United
Nations Capital Development Fund (UNCDF) Special Unit
for Microfinance (SUM): www.undp/org/sum/

United Nations Educational, Scientific and Cultural Organization
(UNESCO) Microfinance Unit: www.unesco.org/opi2/
mfu/mfu.htm